THE RESCUE OF
BELLE *and*
SUNDANCE

BIRGIT STUTZ AND LAWRENCE SCANLAN

THE RESCUE OF BELLE and SUNDANCE

ONE TOWN'S INCREDIBLE RACE TO SAVE TWO ABANDONED HORSES

A MERLOYD LAWRENCE BOOK
DA CAPO PRESS
A MEMBER OF THE PERSEUS BOOKS GROUP

Cataloging-in-Publication data for this book is available from the Library of Congress

First published in the United States as a Merloyd Lawrence Book by Da Capo Press,
a member of the Perseus Books Group, 2012
Reprinted by arrangement with Collins, an imprint of HarperCollins Publishers Ltd.

ISBN 978-0-306-82097-7 (hardcover)
ISBN 978-0-306-82101-1 (e-book)
Library of Congress Control Number 2011938331

Da Capo Press books are available at special discounts for bulk
purchases in the U.S. by corporations, institutions, and other organizations.
For more information, please contact the Special Markets Department
at the Perseus Books Group, 2300 Chestnut Street, Suite 200,
Philadelphia, PA 19103, or call (800) 810-4145, ext. 5000,
or e-mail special.markets@perseusbooks.com.

10 9 8 7 6 5 4 3 2 1

For my grandmother, Hedwig Greutmann,
who passed on to me her love for animals.

And for Belle and Sundance.

"I hope you will fall into good hands; but a horse never knows who may buy him, or who may drive him; it is all a chance for us . . ."
—*Black Beauty* by Anna Sewell, 1877,
a wise mare's advice to her foal

"The greatness of a nation and its moral progress can be judged by the way its animals are treated."
—Mahatma Gandhi, 1869–1948

CONTENTS

Chapter 1

MOUNT RENSHAW

High on the cold, stark mountain, the two horses waited patiently, as horses do.

That fall, the sprawling meadows above the treeline had been resplendent with colour from wildflowers—the red of Indian paintbrush, the yellow of monkey flowers, the deep purple of tall gentians. Rushing creeks would have offered the horses bracing drafts of pure water, and the grass in the alpine meadows, though short, would have been rich and plentiful.

But when the temperatures began to plummet with winter's approach, the grass was soon buried in white, buried beyond the

The alpine below Mount Renshaw, where Belle and Sundance were spotted by local snowmobilers.

horses' pawing, which turned frantic and then ceased altogether. The two horses, a young mare called Belle and a bigger, older gelding called Sundance, each a different shade of brown, stood amid six feet of powdery white snow. The conifers nearby all sagged under the great weight of accumulated snow and ice. Vainly seeking warmth from the other's bony carcass, the two gaunt creatures arranged themselves nose to tail, though little remained of their tails—a sure sign they were starving. Each horse had gnawed away at the other's tail, desperately looking for a source of protein.

The view from this mountaintop is one of unparalleled beauty, and it may be that horses, like humans, appreciate such grandeur. But not when the eyes stare blankly, the belly is long empty, the ribs and hip bones are plain to see.

A great many blizzards had already whipped through this section of the Rocky Mountains, and a cruel blanket of snow and ice lay on the horses' backs. They were shivering and waiting for the inevitable.

~

The story of Belle and Sundance features a cast of many characters—some of whom played crucial roles in what happened next. For various reasons, I became one of the voices of the story that unfolded just before Christmas of 2008.

I was born in Zurich, Switzerland, in 1971. I spent the first two years of my life in Thalwil, a town near Zurich, but grew up in a village called Richterswil, on Lake Zurich. I have always loved animals and, at age thirteen, began taking riding lessons. I bought my first horse, Machlon, a somewhat crazed Russian–Arabian who had been abused and whom I still have, when I was in my early twenties. After high school, I studied English literature, English linguistics, journalism and North American history, but I always harboured what I called "a cowboy dream"—to own a ranch and live in the mountains of Western Canada.

I am now living that dream with my husband, Marc Lavigne. At our eighty-acre Falling Star Ranch near McBride in the Robson Valley of British Columbia, I train and breed horses—mostly part-bred Arabians—and teach riders.

What put me up on Mount Renshaw was simple. I cannot stand to see animals suffering, and it seems I am not alone.

McBride is a small town in the wide, flat valley near Mount Renshaw in northeastern B.C. Just a century ago, most men in the valley made their living as trappers and loggers, and their families lived in log cabins. Sawmills sprouted up to meet the demands of the new railroad that came through in 1912. Timber was needed not only for the Grand Trunk Pacific's rail ties but also for sidewalks, fences, houses and stores in the villages that would dot the rail line. Tête Jaune Cache. Valemount. Dunster. Dome Creek. Crescent Spur. Croydon. Lamming Mills. And the biggest, McBride, named after a British Columbia premier of the early twentieth century and today home to seven hundred souls. All of these towns' names are rooted in the rich pioneer history of the Robson Valley. Tête

Jaune, meaning Yellow Head, remembers the long blond hair of a local Métis guide who crossed the Rocky Mountains in 1819 in the service of the Hudson's Bay Company. Mount Renshaw is named for a trapper who worked out of McBride in the early 1900s.

The valley sits on the edge of an interior cedar–hemlock rainforest, the world's only inland temperate rainforest—one that thrives thanks to the west winds that bring ample rain in summer and snow in winter to fuel forest growth. Some of the trees around McBride are more than a thousand years old. The forest, with the help of sturdy horses, has long offered a living here—though never an easy one. Loggers felled the giant Douglas firs and cedars and hemlocks in winter, horses hauled the logs to the mills, millworkers cut them into lumber, and the trains took it all away. For a century, that's what made the valley tick.

But the mills' day had come and, just recently, all but gone. Decisions made in capitals and corporate boardrooms far to the east, limp demand for building material in the wake of a real estate crash to the south, bank failures there and pinched pockets everywhere have all rocked the valley. Jobs in the forests around McBride have become scarce. Tourism, for better or for worse, has taken over. Hikers and horseback riders, hunters and fishers, kayakers and whitewater rafters, mountain bikers and birdwatchers find a haven here in summer. In winter, heli-skiers, cross-country skiers and recreational snowmobilers find the area irresistible. The air is pure, the waters pristine, the sense of space and freedom keenly felt.

"We live in beauty," a friend of mine once told me, and there are takers in every season, winter most of all.

Logan Jeck and Leif Gunster were born and bred in these mountains and have been friends all their lives. They cherish snowmobiling and the outdoor life, and with work so scarce, they joke darkly about having more time than money. But for all the changes inflicted on the valley, one constant is the instinct to assist those in distress. Up here, "Help thy neighbour" is a commandment bred in the bone. We wouldn't survive otherwise. Leif calls it "the McBride mentality." He has worked in northern Alberta in the fast-cash, oil-fuelled economy, but while the money is good, the life is not. He couldn't wait to get back home to the Robson Valley, where people actually look out for one another.

Leif knows, and loves, the territory. A skilled sledder, he drives an Arctic Cat 800, a powerful snow machine that generates 150 horsepower and hits a top speed of 140 kilometres an hour. When it's available, Leif finds work as a logger in the McBride area and, in the fall, as a hunting guide on horseback in the Yukon. A compactly built and strong young man with light brown hair, blue eyes and chiselled features, Leif is like so many around here: comfortable with horsepower in all its forms.

As for Logan, the name Jeck is a recognizable one in the community. Logan's great-grandfather came to the area in 1924 from New Sarepta in central Alberta, a fact remembered in Jeck Road, which runs off the highway outside McBride. In December 2008, Logan was, by all accounts, a well-mannered, soft-spoken young man. Blond and tall with an athletic build, he worked in the forest as a faller and had done some heli-logging, but like Leif, he went to where the work was. Although Logan had grown up in a family of horse people, he had never really taken to horses. He preferred his horsepower in a machine.

But Logan knew, and Leif knew, that a mountain can be a treacherous place any time of the year, doubly so in winter. Blizzards strike without warning and the terrain is dangerously steep in places. There is a knack to driving a snow machine in the mountains, and even seasoned snowmobilers get into trouble on the Renshaw, as some locals call it. The uninitiated might think that a machine built to run over snow couldn't possibly get stuck in the stuff, but many sledders have discovered the hard way that in several feet of fresh powder, sleds may float, or sink, according to the skill, luck and circumstances of the driver.

Mount Renshaw boasts the largest maintained sledding area in North America. In early December of 2008, the mountain was doing its usual job of accommodating thousands of snowmobilers without anyone feeling crowded or pinched. The views, as always, were spellbinding and even the risks of the mountain, it seemed, possessed a certain allure. The local search and rescue team had spent three successive nights rescuing sledders in the backcountry; when snowstorms lashed the mountain yet again, the men were too spent to go out. They called on Logan and Leif, then twenty and twenty-one respectively, who generously agreed to relieve them. Visitors from Alberta had gotten their snowmobiles mired in deep snow and had walked to a warming cabin nearby. The search and rescue crew had gotten the sledders out, but the tasks of locating and towing their machines off the mountain still remained.

In a typical winter on Mount Renshaw, ten metres of snow will fall, and the base will settle in at more than three metres deep. That December 15, with the temperature hovering around minus thirty degrees Celsius, a light flurry had added to the lovely pile. Logan and Leif were searching below Mount Renshaw, two kilometres from the warming cabin. They had pushed past a high ridge called "the saddle," which overlooks a massively wide expanse called "the bowl," much favoured by sledders. Just before noon on that bitterly cold morning, Logan and Leif were down in the bowl scouting for the lost snow machines. Noticing what they took to be moose in a gully near the warming cabin just above the treeline, they stopped. There was something odd about the sighting. The moose, if moose they were, stood frightfully still and their heads hung low. Curious, Leif and Logan advanced.

When the two men grew close, they realized they had come upon two grossly emaciated horses. Logan knows his way around a horse and had worked for outfitters; his father, uncle and sister are all horse people. His gut response to the stricken animals was revulsion. In a starving horse, the bones are so prominent that the skeleton appears to be that of a larger horse. The tail is quiet, the head is low, the ears still, the eyes dull. These two horses had ceased to interact with their environment; gone were hope and expectation. Breathing was a chore. Their sad and low-hanging heads spoke of their despair.

The two horses had packed down the snow and made a claustrophobic enclosure, maybe twelve feet square, with six-foot-high snow walls all around. They were trapped near the summit of a 2,400-metre-high mountain in the dead of winter. The horses were alive, though barely. Logan took a cheese stick from his pocket and gave it to the mare, who accepted it feebly.

By Leif's estimation, the horses hadn't eaten in a month. Ribs and hipbones prominent, backbones in sharp relief, they looked more like skinny cows than horses. Leif took no notice of their height or colour or markings, only their sad, drawn faces that seemed to beg for mercy. The two men felt helpless and angry. Leif wished he'd been carrying a pistol or a rifle. He would have shot the horses then and there to end their suffering.

The men well knew how easy it is to lose a horse in the bush (a lightning flash or the scent of a cougar can cause a horse to panic and flee, and some horses take off out of mischief), but still, the sight of two horses so high up the mountain confounded them. Logan and Leif had also heard about heartless outfitters who simply released unwanted mounts into the wilderness and forgot about them. The question of how these two horses had become stranded on a mountaintop in winter would remain unanswered for the moment.

The larger question, the one that demanded an immediate answer, was this: What were they going to do about these starving horses?

Chapter 2
LOST HORSES

Belle and Sundance were pack horses, and to begin to understand how they came to be marooned in winter near the top of a snowbound mountain, it's important to know something about horses in general and pack horses in particular.

Every horse herd is also a hierarchy, and whether there are two or twenty horses in that herd, each knows precisely where he or she fits. By tests of courage or small signs (a pinning of ears, a kick—or the threat of one), dominance is determined, and the bold and the timid and those in between neatly arrange themselves. If, in a paddock, horse number two, say, were to drink or dine before horse number one had done so, the latter might have something to say about that. If horse number twenty pulled rank in that fashion, there would be hell to pay.

One of the many things I love about horse society is that horses know their place, and once that place is established, they tend toward peaceful coexistence and even mutual aid. Two horse chums in a field will align themselves head to tail on a hot summer day so they can swat flies on each other's face with their tails or gently groom each other along the flanks with their teeth. Horses buddy up and form allegiances, and sometimes these connections are intense. Typically, high-ranking horses pair up with each other, and low-ranking horses do the same. Belle and Sundance were both dominant horses. In a cruel twist, the tight bond between them would contribute to the grim circumstance in which they found themselves on Mount Renshaw.

Another kind of hierarchy exists among horses, according to task—though this ranking is by human, not equine, design. At the top of the heap are the sport horses, the ones that may command millions of dollars when they are bought and sold: sleek thoroughbreds of the racetrack, powerful warm-blooded show jumpers, graceful dressage horses, cutting and reining horses that rule western horse shows. On this scale, school horses—the ones used to help teach novices how to ride—are well down the line.

But at the very bottom of that ranking are pack horses. They need not possess speed or agility or understand any of the subtle forms of communication that pass between rider and horse. A pack horse needs just a few credentials: a strong back, a willingness to follow the one ahead, a calm and gentle disposition and, finally, a sure-footedness in rugged and steep terrain.

The pack horse line is ancient. Humans began to ride horses at least six thousand years ago, but evidence suggests horses were penned or tethered as early as thirty thousand years ago. It's a good bet that the first horses encountered by humans were hunted for meat and that long before that first human got on the back of that first horse, horses and mules, donkeys and ponies were carrying loads. Where roads were poor or non-existent, the pack horse conveyed goods to market. In the Old West, pack horse trains were sometimes a hundred horses long. Even today, forest and park rangers, surveyors, miners, ranchers and outfitters all over North America use them. And pack horses continue to work throughout the developing world. In the Rockies, they power hunting expeditions, camping trips and geological forays. The pack horse, in short, has never fallen out of favour.

The pack horse's treatment depends largely on circumstance and the conscience and means of its owner. Pity the horse whose owners are poor—poor in sympathy for horses, poor in their ability to fathom the ways of horses, poor in the ordinary sense of that word. If a family routinely goes hungry, their horse likely suffers the same fate. Even a horse of high breeding can come to know neglect, but pack horses such as Belle and Sundance—widely viewed as the cheapest and most expendable of their kind—are the most vulnerable.

~

Taking pack horses into the Rocky Mountains of northeastern British Columbia—especially the rugged western slope where I live—is not for the faint of heart. Without years of experience, anyone planning such an expedition would do well to either hire a good guide, travel with someone experienced or, at the very least, read up on the subject.

Most outfitters in the Robson Valley have read what they call "the packer's bible." *Horses, Hitches and Rocky Trails*, written by Joe Back in 1959, is a remarkable little 117-page book—remarkable not least for its detailed and often wry illustrations, its homespun wisdom and for the fact that its advice is still followed almost to the letter by outfitters more than fifty years later. If horses are some-times dangerous, mountains are more so, and the combination of the two can be deadly. "The lack of two or three cave men tools and a few simple precautions," wrote Back, "can sometimes bring modern men to disaster and even death."

Leading pack horses in the mountains requires experience and a complicated set of skills. A simple omission, like forgetting to bring an axe to make a fire if need be, may prove fatal. You have to know your knots—the diamond hitch (single and double), the basket hitch, the half-hitched diamond. You have to know about saddles—the Decker, the sawbuck, the Spanish. You have to know about panniers (baskets slung on either side of the pack horse), slings and much else.

And even if you were to pack a horse perfectly, with a keen eye for balance and weight, the job doesn't end there. The breast collar has to be just so, so the load won't shift backward when the horse goes uphill. As the horse loses weight from all this labour, the cinch loosens. Working also makes him thirsty, and when he fills up on water at every creek he passes (sometimes just so he can take a break), his belly expands, tightening the cinch again. Supreme vigilance and careful horsemanship are a must. "A horse gets to eat in his spare time, if any," observed Back, "and if you push him beyond reason you walk home, and that poor devil ends up in a coyote or a can."

~

Belle and Sundance's journey up Mount Renshaw began on September 12, 2008. Frank Mackay, a lawyer in Edmonton, some four hundred kilometres to the east as the crow flies, was bringing supplies to a friend who was hiking the Great Divide, which aligns pretty well with the B.C.–Alberta border. It seemed like a simple enough task for a man who had owned horses for a decade and who likely saw himself as a horseman. But things went wrong, very wrong, on that trip.

The vast alpine area of Mount Renshaw.

The sixty-three-year-old was riding his saddle horse, and leading Belle and Sundance, who dutifully carried their loads. Sundance was a fourteen-year-old gelding, a sorrel (a horse with a reddish brown coat and a mane and tail the same colour or flaxen); Belle was a three-year-old mare, a bay (dark brown in colour with black points—mane, tail, lower legs). This was Mackay's first solo mountain expedition, and he quickly discovered the many challenges: on the way to Beaver Dam Pass, he got lost, veering east when he should have gone west. The weather, as it often does in the Canadian Rockies, turned foul and cold. And a brewing mutiny by his two pack horses finally erupted.

What befell the group high in the alpine that day was not weather but unruly and rough terrain. Bog, to be precise. In previous years, crews had cut trees to widen a snowmobile trail, and all the deadfall lying in low and wet areas pinched and grabbed at the horses' legs. The horses were soon exhausted, then stuck, and the man leading them struggled to extricate them. "It was like pick-up sticks in there, with muskeg in between," Mackay would later report. "This stuff was just muck."

Mackay had failed to heed one of Joe Back's rules:

> On bad trails, across deep streams, bog holes,
> slide rock, and along canyon trails, it's safer to

drive the pack horses loose, and let them pick
their own way around bad and chancy sections.
A lot of the time the pack animal shows far better
judgement than the packer . . . two-legged fools
rush in where four-legged angels fear to tread.

Eventually, Mackay and his horses made it past the Renshaw warming cabin, where again the two pack horses got mired in bog.

Belle and Sundance had had enough. Even after they were relieved of their loads and untethered, they refused to follow their master's lead. The pack horses had lost faith. The mare was spent by her travails, and the stronger gelding, though able to, would not leave her side. The bond between the two was too strong.

Frank Mackay spent the night of September 12 on Mount Renshaw with all three horses, and the following morning he abandoned his camping equipment on the mountainside and rode out on his saddle horse, telling himself that the two pack horses would soon enough find their way to a logging road and from there to the main valley, where someone would see them and report them. He also informed the Royal Canadian Mounted Police detachment in McBride, which serves as the local police, in case the loose horses were spotted coming down the mountain.

The man had fully expected the pack horses to head for the valley within a few days. This was a reasonable expectation in ordinary circumstances, local outfitters would later confirm. But the expected didn't occur, probably because the horses would have associated descending the mountain with revisiting that miserable bog.

The gelding and the mare were left alone on the mountain, but they were also free. Mount Renshaw, for the time being, proved a blissful place for Belle and Sundance to be.

Chapter 3

HORSE HEAVEN, HORSE HELL

For weeks that fall, Belle and Sundance would have revelled in their newfound freedom. The horses could graze to their hearts' content in those yawning alpine meadows; they could nap in the sun in the afternoon and play when play was called for. At night, they would have slept, although one of them would have remained alert, testing the winds for any sign of wolf, cougar or bear.

Dark-chocolate brown in colour, Belle bore a star on her forehead, almost a stripe, and had small eyes that suggested she might be scheming. The young mare was the saucier and more sure-footed of the two horses and would surely have pushed the envelope with her heavier, more senior companion. Teased him, nipped him, tested his patience.

Sundance, a chestnut with three white stockings, sported a wide blaze on his head and large, pretty eyes. Although calm and laid-back, the gelding was clearly the boss of the pair. At 16.2 hands, he also had size in his favour. (A hand, in reference to horses, refers to height. Our forebears used the adult hand, four inches across, to measure the height of a horse. So a 16.2-hand horse stands sixty-six inches from the ground to the withers, the highest part of the back. Belle, at 15.2, was sixty-two inches from ground to withers.) Lanky and somewhat stiff, Sundance would get pushy with both horses and humans and gravitated to the leadership of any herd he joined.

On the mountain, Belle and Sundance were camped in majestic territory. Geographical place names here sound almost boastful: White Falls, Falls of the Pool, Emperor Falls, Rainbow Falls, Tumbling Glacier, the Valley of a Thousand Falls and the Emperor Face of Mount Robson. Mount Robson itself is the stunning high point of the Canadian Rockies, and climbers attempting to reach its almost four-thousand-metre summit are rebuffed by weather ninety per cent of the time. Those who make it, though, glory in views that extend one hundred kilometres in every direction. I have never been up there, but hikers rave about the mountain's vast

*Sundance (left) and Belle enjoying their freedom in the
Renshaw area, mid-September 2008.*

meadows and many lakes, as well as the glaciers—the longest one,
twelve hundred metres in length—that spill into the aquamarine
waters of Berg Lake.

In mid-September, not long after their owner had left them, one
such hiker spotted the two horses. Glen Stanley will modestly say he
has done a bit of hiking: he has twice climbed Mount Robson and
has hiked to Berg Lake a staggering seventy-six times. But despite
all that experience over his seventy years, what Glen saw on that
early fall day jarred him. He was hiking with his dog Badge when

he chanced upon two horses gambolling high in the alpine about two kilometres north of the Renshaw cabin. "There's a ridge running south and east from the peak of Mount Renshaw separating two meadows," said Glen. "This is up high, where the last grass is. The place is a small pocket of short grass, with water. I'm not a horse person, but I would think it would be an ideal place for them."

The horses shook their heads at the hiker and his dog. First the horses came to them, then they scattered, then they returned. Using a telephoto lens, Glen took pictures of them. The horses in the photos look fat and sassy and happy and, with their glistening coats, in perfect health. They wore bells at their necks, as is common for horses taken into the mountains—to give fair warning to bears and to help a rider retrieve them should they spook and flee. But there was no owner to be seen. The whole thing puzzled Glen. What were two horses doing way up there alone?

Not long after, as he sat in the meadow eating his lunch, Glen saw a helicopter fly overhead. He assumed it was part of a search team looking for two lost horses. But when he later called Yellowhead Helicopters, which has a base in the nearby village of Valemount, he was told that what he had observed was a routine flight to check out a stand of timber. So Glen called the RCMP, who gave him the answer he was looking for. A man on his way to Grande Cache, Alberta, had had two of his horses bog down on Mount Renshaw.

Having learned that the animals' presence on the mountain was known, Glen assumed the owner would return for them very soon. Horses are valuable animals; no one would just leave them there, especially with winter coming.

~

Aside from Glen, few in the Robson Valley knew there were horses running free in the alpine that fall. One exception was Wes Phillips. Wes started working as a guide in the mountains at the age of seventeen, almost thirty years before, and to him, the lost horses presented an opportunity. He had just come back from a trip to the Yukon when "the old moccasin telegraph," as he calls word of mouth in the mountains, told him that two horses were loose on the north fork of the Blackwater River below Mount Renshaw. "There's an unwritten law in the mountains," he says. "Someone callous enough to leave any unbranded horses over four up in the mountains . . . it's finders keepers." Four is deemed to be the age a wild horse would leave its dam.

Twice, once at Thanksgiving in mid-October and again a week later, Wes drove up the logging road—formally called McKale Forest Service Road but locally also known as Blackwater River Road. He parked at kilometre twenty-six and then searched for the horses on foot. The weather grew nasty as he went that first time, with cold rain turning to snow, resulting in a four-inch dump. The second time, a foot of snow covered the ground, putting an end to Wes's search.

Wes had reason to believe that even high atop a mountain in winter's grip, horses can find ways to survive. "Horses can surprise you with their fortitude," he says. "One time I had a horse hit by a train. Half his face was torn off. I thought, Better put him down. But in six months it had healed over. Another time, a horse of mine was attacked by wolves. He was just a little horse, but he got away. He couldn't walk for four or five months, but he made it."

Wes felt certain that the two horses were alive and somewhere on the mountain, but where was anybody's guess.

～

When October turned to November up on Mount Renshaw, everything changed for Belle and Sundance. The snow began to fall with greater regularity, and the nights got colder. The banquets of rich alpine grass the two horses had enjoyed in the fall became just memories. The verdant mountain meadows, which had offered the horses a freedom the likes of which they had never experienced, gradually transformed into something else: a cold, white prison.

In mid-November, snowmobilers took photos of the horses running in the powder and posted them on SnowandMud.com, a popular Internet forum for sledders in the valley and indeed all over the continent. Sadly, the fact that horses ran loose on the mountain without food or shelter failed to register; most likely, the posters and viewers of the photos assumed that the owner or the authorities had the situation well in hand.

And so more time passed. As the snow got deeper, the horses—now weak from hunger—ultimately realized the futility of moving at all.

Frank Mackay made two attempts to retrieve his horses. Some six weeks after leaving them, during the last week in October, he rode up Mount Renshaw on a saddle horse borrowed from a local outfitter named Stan Walchuk. But heavy snowfall on the mountain confounded his search effort.

Some six weeks after that, on December 5, Mackay returned. This time he knew the whereabouts of Belle and Sundance thanks to some young snowmobilers—relatives of one of his clients—who had happened upon the horses two days before. Once he got the call, "I packed my gear and loaded up and headed out there,"

Mackay later told me in a telephone interview I did for a local newspaper, the *Valley Sentinel*, in nearby Valemount.

Belle and Sundance's owner was on a snowmobile, not a horse this time, and he was hauling hay, oats and alfalfa pellets to feed his two pack horses. Having sought help, he was accompanied by a sledder who knew the terrain of Mount Renshaw. But once again, a dump of snow stymied any rescue, and the two men lost their way for a time. "We couldn't even see the bottom of the mountain," Mackay told me. "We didn't know which way was out."

On their way up the mountain's bumpy trail, the hay fell off the sled. The loss of the hay was perhaps telling of the men's unpreparedness or the rugged landscape, or both. In any case, although Mackay eventually found Belle and Sundance, the horses got no hay.

"They were pretty pathetic looking," Mackay told me. "They were skin and bone." A far cry from the plump and playful creatures Glen Stanley had stumbled upon almost three months earlier.

A starving horse will start to draw on stores of fat and carbohydrates to produce energy for metabolism—blood flow, brain function, the normal workings of the body. That process in a healthy horse begins with nutrients derived from food, but when food is no longer available, the body looks for other sources of protein—muscle mass, vital organs. A horse can lose thirty per cent of its body weight and rebound, a testament to the equine will to survive. We know from the testimony of humans that hunger pangs are very real and that the process of starvation also involves headaches and dizziness—not to mention mental anguish. I imagine that it's much the same for horses. These two pack horses were domesticated animals, used to having their needs met for them. This is the nature of the contract between humans and horses. "I'll work for you," the horse as much has said. "I'll carry you into war, I'll race for you, I'll leap those fences, I'll help round up those cattle, I'll transport you and your goods. But I'm counting on you to keep me fed and watered and sheltered from the storm."

Mackay tried to give the emaciated horses the food he had brought—thirty pounds of oats and alfalfa pellets and eight litres of Gatorade. He had thought to use the power drink to restore the horses' electrolyte levels because by then hunger and thirst would have been playing havoc with their blood chemistry. So he poured Gatorade onto the oats and tried to force the rest down the horses' throats through a funnel attached to a hose.

"They were vomiting it up because they couldn't hold it," Mackay said later, adding that some of the food came out through their nostrils. "I was trying to give them some strength," he said. "I fed them as best I could."

No doubt he did. Apparently, however, he was unaware that

horses are not physically capable of vomiting. Belle and Sundance were simply balking at being fed in this way. A more knowledgeable horseman never would have attempted such an unconventional feeding method. "Tubing," as it's called, is sometimes used to administer mineral oil to a horse with a gastrointestinal problem, but the process requires experience and a deft hand. Given the poor state of the horses, the sugar in the Gatorade could have provoked spasmodic or cramp colic or colic itself—a painful twist or blockage in the bowels and the leading cause of premature death in horses.

In their owner's estimation, the horses were too weak to walk out, and the deep snow wouldn't have allowed them passage anyway. Mackay left them the rest of the oats and alfalfa, a kind of last supper. He then took off the bells they were wearing and tearfully bade his horses farewell. The horses were being left for dead. Mackay had brought no gun to dispatch them, and, as he subsequently put it in an interview with me, "That's all I could do. I made every effort I thought I could . . . physically or humanly, and after that you have to make a tough decision. I didn't have a gun, and I wasn't going to slit their throats. Even if I had a gun, I don't think I could have shot them. Everybody thinks euthanasia would have been the best thing. I had nothing to kill them with. I didn't go up there to kill them. I let nature take its course."

Mackay perhaps assumed the two pack horses to be far closer to death than they were. If so, he vastly underestimated the resilience of his horses and their will to live.

When later questioned about his ultimate decision to abandon the animals, Mackay appeared to blame the horses themselves for their misfortune. "Horses are like teenagers," he said. "If they can get into trouble, they will get into trouble."

Dumbfounded, I inquired, "Why didn't you ask for help?"

"I doubt people would have helped a stranger," he replied.

Driving home to Edmonton that day after his failed rescue attempt, Mackay was involved in an accident near Mount Robson and rolled his truck and trailer. As he later told reporters, he had sustained a concussion and a deep gash to the top of his head, along with other injuries that left him unable to work.

Horses have no word for abandonment, but surely Belle and Sundance felt it. The long nights, especially, must have been excruciating as the temperatures progressively dipped on that mountain and the cold settled into their bones.

Chapter 4

SENDING OUT AN SOS

McBride is a typical small town in Western Canada, with wide streets and faux facades, with angled parking and no building higher than two storeys. Encased in boulders, the welcome sign at the village entrance on Main Street features a black steam locomotive: the heritage railway station in town has been preserved and highlighted as a focal point—it matters that the train still stops here. The town's fire hydrants are all gaily painted—some powder blue with Aboriginal art, some with happy Dalmatians, some with blue-eyed railwaymen. Smile, the art proclaims. Pause and smile.

There's a quirkiness to the Robson Valley that I love. In a field not far from the Dunster General Store, someone has parked a TV set on the hood of a rusting car—a homemade sculpture as welcoming as a wink. One long driveway near the hamlet features a car bench-seat strapped to a cedar-rail fence, and this strange pairing, too, makes me smile. On the outside wall of our tack shed, we've stuck a black rotary phone—another found object given licence to amuse.

In the villages of the valley, there is no cinema: if you want to watch a movie, you rent a DVD and watch it at home or you catch movie night at the high school, McBride Secondary. Bingo takes place at the Legion Hall, the New Year's dance at the Elks Hall. The annual fishing derby is a big deal, as are curling, hockey and figure skating, the Valemountain Days celebration in Valemount in May, the Pioneer Days celebration in McBride in June, the Robson Valley Fall Fair in McBride in September and the Valemount Winter Festival.

The mighty Fraser River, the rail line and the Robson Valley all follow the same trajectory—from the northwest to the southeast. Eons ago, the river would have overflowed its banks and cast up rich alluvial soil on the valley floor. Now just about every foot of available land on the Robson Valley floor is cultivated. The town of McBride sits on the river's south bank, set back a respectful distance from the river and the raging torrents unleashed each spring when snow on the mountains melts.

The Robson Valley may look paradisical, but of course it's not. Because of high unemployment, the men and women who live here are forever heading elsewhere—to the oil fields of Alberta or the Middle East or points in-between—for work. Not all marriages survive such separations and stresses, and divorce and spousal abuse are issues here, as they are everywhere. And as I write these words, a rogue bear has for weeks been slaughtering cattle in the valley, including those in the fields right next to my own.

Still, when the setting sun casts a pink glow on the snow-covered mountain passes in early summer, when a healthy foal arrives one day at a friend's ranch and the next day at mine, when the cotton-woods are flashing new leaves and spring rain leaves the air smelling sweet, when our hummingbird feeders need air traffic controllers and the mountain creeks are rushing headlong to the Fraser, on such days I really do believe that I live in paradise.

"Let the mountains move you," it says below Valemount's welcome sign built of massive fir logs, and we are moved.

~

Somewhere up on those mountains roamed two horses. Glen Stanley knew about their presence there, as did Wes Phillips and the snowmobilers who had posted the horses' photos on the sledding website.

The view from the horses' snowy pen, just below Mount Renshaw.

The mechanism that spreads the news of unusual events in small towns now kicked into gear.

And as tends to happen, a grain of truth got stretched and distorted as it flitted from one source to the next. One rumour had it that three horses, not two, had been spotted on the mountainside and that one horse was hobbled. Someone reported seeing horse tracks on the logging road further down the mountain—or were they moose tracks? Another rumour had it on good authority that the two lost pack horses were dead. Finally, a story circulating in a schoolyard claimed that a good Samaritan, a woman, had taken it upon herself to helicopter some hay up to the starving horses.

Ray Long, having heard tell of the horse sightings on the Renshaw, knew where to go for reliable information. On the morning of Tuesday, December 9, he drove into town and walked into Spin Drift Power Sports, the place in McBride where locals head to get their snow machine fixed or replaced if need be. If there was any hope of finding and helping horses lost on that mountain, Ray knew snowmobiles and snowmobilers would have to play a part.

A stocky man in his mid-seventies with a round, ruddy face and bushy eyebrows over light blue eyes, Ray is known to often be up to mischief. Here's a sample: Luella (everyone calls her Lu), Ray's wife, is a tall thin woman who still looks fit (she competed as a sprinter and hurdler in the 1952 Olympics). But with age, of course, come ailments and stiffness. Some of the townspeople can recite the story of what happened when Lu had a Reiki therapist over for a treatment. Operating on the theory that the body emanates energy fields, Reiki involves the sometimes rapid passing of the therapist's hands over the patient's body. Ray walked into the room and saw the therapist making flicking motions to the floor with her fingers. He asked her what she was doing.

"I'm taking all the negative energy away from Lu," the therapist answered.

"Well, for Christ's sake," Ray exclaimed. "I'll get a bucket. Don't flick that stuff on the floor!"

A kind and compassionate man, Ray finds great solace and satisfaction in his work, rising at dawn each day as he has all his life. His uniform is a collared western shirt and Wrangler jeans held up by a pair of bright red Carhartt suspenders (or "spenders," as he calls them). On his six-hundred-acre farm, he runs seventy-five head of cattle, stables his older daughter's three horses and operates the local large-animal pound—a place that houses stray horses and cattle until their owners can be located.

In his younger days, Ray was a fine horseman who learned a lot from his father and Pat Smith, a cowboy pal of his dad's. The two men had rodeoed with Pete Knight, the so-called king of the cowboys. Knight worked on a ranch at Crossfield, north of Calgary, and became a world champion bronc rider in the 1930s. He was killed in 1937—trampled at a rodeo in California.

Ray will concede that "mountains make thin soup"—that is, you can't live on scenery. But if he hasn't travelled much, it's because he loves this place and never wants to leave it. Ray has a long history and fond memories of trekking into the mountains with his horses. Handsomely framed and blown-up colour photographs of Ray leading pack horses across a mountain stream enjoy pride of place on his living room wall.

"I like pack horses," he once told me. "They did a lot of work for me." If there were indeed horses on the Renshaw, he wanted to know so he could do something about it. Lu would echo that thought. "You can't be a farmer," she says, "and not have a soft spot for animals."

That day at Spin Drift Ray learned that there were horses up on the mountain, apparently abandoned, and they were starving. Angry, he got on the phone. Spread the word was his first thought.

Ray Long called his friend Reg Marek, who had likewise spent many years trekking into the mountains with horses. Reg—a tall man of medium build, with glasses that give him a slightly scholarly look—has been taking pack horses into the mountains for forty years. Like Ray, Reg wears many hats in the valley: he is a cattle rancher, he boards horses, he is a trained farrier, he runs a tack shop (Kicking Horse Saddlery) for which he crafts gorgeous, custom-made western saddles, he is a farm-seed seller, and he is the local brand inspector (the strict tracking of cattle—birth, sale, death—helps control disease, prevent poaching and ensure that stolen or stray animals get back to their rightful owners). When Ray told Reg about the abandoned horses, Reg in turn called Monika Brown.

It was shortly before nine o'clock that same evening that the phone rang at my house. It was Monika, my best friend, and she was distraught. "Reg just called and told me that there are two starving, abandoned horses in the Renshaw area," she said. "Reg got it from Ray, who heard they were in very rough shape and possibly even dead by now."

I had a long list of questions for Monika. "Why are they up there? Who's the owner? *Where's* the owner?"

Monika didn't have the answers, but she was perhaps the first to act to find them. Cute and short in stature, Monika is a firebrand who won't hesitate to write frank letters to the editor or to speak her mind—especially where the abuse of animals is concerned. "I'm an animal lover," Monika says. "I once spent hours hacking into the ice to rescue a duck. It's just a given."

Sixteen years ago, the two of us were working at a ranch in Hinton, Alberta, where our friendship formed and flourished. She loves horses as much as I do. Monika, her husband, Tim, and his twelve-year-old son, Justin, live on a small acreage outside McBride. She owns four horses, along with a dog and several cats.

When Monika heard about those horses up on the mountain, she knew she had to help. The first thing she did was recruit her husband. Tim Brown called Barry Walline, president of the McBride Big Country Snowmobile Association and a member of the Robson Valley Search and Rescue team. Barry told Tim he had seen what looked to be horse tracks on the logging road, at kilometre twelve.

The next day, December 10, Monika took a day off work—she's a secretary at McBride Auto Body & Towing—and she and Tim, home for a few days from his job in the Alberta oil fields, rented a snowmobile from Spin Drift, which sits next door to Monika's employer.

"Conditions for sledding are really bad," warned the shop's co-owner, Glenn Daykin, who cited fresh snow in the mountains and unseasonably warm weather. This was perhaps a bit of good news for Belle and Sundance, but bad news for their would-be rescuers.

Despite the warning, Monika and Tim decided to give it a try. At kilometre twenty-four on the logging road, they ran into the man contracted to maintain the sledding trails on Mount Renshaw and two areas nearby. He advised them that they'd reached the end of the groomed trail and should go no further, adding that even veteran riders on more powerful snowmobiles than theirs were getting stuck in the deep and heavy snow. A disappointed Monika and Tim turned back. They'd seen no sign of horses, but they had found hay on the trail at kilometre twelve on the logging road. The couple didn't know what to make of that. Had some sledders heard about the horses and brought them hay? Was this the owner's doing? Had he brought the horses partway out and fed them along the way? How long had that hay been there? All these questions . . . and no answers.

Later that same day, Monika called local outfitter Stan Walchuk after hearing that he might have information about the lost horses. Stan would only say that the owner was a fellow named Frank and that he lived in Alberta and had come to Stan for help a while back. In Stan's opinion, the owner wasn't negligent, just too inexperienced to be in the mountains with horses by himself. Finally, Stan told Monika that the owner had been up to see the horses the weekend before, that they were beyond rescuing, and he assumed that the owner had done the right thing and put the horses out of their misery.

The following day, Monika dropped in to Glenn Daykin's shop to get the latest information. There were no updated sightings, but there was a promising lead in solving the mystery of who owned the lost horses. A sledder from Alberta had called Daykin early in December, reported the lost horses and asked if local sledders could get back to him if they spotted the animals. He had apparently accompanied the pack horses' owner on a snowmobile in an attempt to extricate them on December 5.

When Monika finally got through to that sledder on Friday, December 12, he confirmed the story. "The horses were in terrible shape," he told Monika on the telephone. "Rest assured. They're dead by now."

"Did you put the horses down?" she asked him.

"No," he replied. "We didn't have a gun." Monika asked him if there was ever any plan to go back to euthanize the horses, but he didn't answer the question.

Monika had called the man out of curiosity, hoping that he had some answers about the abandoned horses. She took notes as they talked, for she intended to pass on to Ray and Reg and me and anyone else who shared an interest whatever information she managed to collect. But Monika grew frustrated as the exchange continued. It must have been clear that at that time of year the horses would be in rough shape—but they brought no gun? She asked several times for the name of the owner, but the sledder declined to share it. "I don't want to judge the man," he told her. "Besides, it wouldn't help the horses any more if the guy got into trouble. I saw the owner crying over his horses. I think he's suffered enough."

Even though he wouldn't name names, he did fill in a few gaps in the horses' story. Without going into specifics, he told Monika that Belle and Sundance's owner had made two elaborate attempts to save his horses, had done everything he could—and that there were a lot of other animals suffering in the world.

"People are more concerned about the welfare of animals than they are about the welfare of people," he said.

This is a commonly expressed response to the suffering of animals, and Monika finds it bizarre. Surely every act of generosity has its own genesis? Where is it written that showing kindness to animals comes at the expense of kindness to humans? Helping is helping. Period. Had there been people stuck up on that mountain, Monika and a great many others in the valley would have felt the same instinct to help.

"I grew up on a farm," he told Monika, "and I've seen lots of animals die." He said he himself had once shot starving animals on a neighbouring farm when their owner could no longer afford to feed them.

Monika returned to her question. "Should the horses have been euthanized to stop their suffering?"

"Yes," came the reply.

"Then why wasn't that taken care of?"

Silence.

Though she was doing her best to remain outwardly polite, Monika was seething inside. "I hope you can sleep at night," she said.

"I sleep just fine, don't worry."

~

That same day, as Monika put it, "All hell broke loose." Temperatures rose, then plummeted. At least two feet of fresh snow fell on Mount Renshaw, thwarting the efforts of snowmobilers trying to deliver propane cylinders to the warming cabin. The perilous conditions resulted in numerous reports of sledders getting stuck or hurt. Members of the Robson Valley Search and Rescue team were called upon when an Alberta snowmobiler was seriously injured near the warming cabin on Mount Lucille—another popular snowmobiling area west of McBride.

The news of the blizzard pretty well, but not entirely, crushed any hope of rescuing those horses. Those of us in their corner feared that their chance of survival was slim in that snow and cold. And even if, somehow, the horses remained alive, the dump of snow surely cut off any access to them. Still, none of us would accept assumptions. If the horses were dead, we needed evidence of that fact.

That night I drove to Valemount to attend a Christmas party put on by the *Valley Sentinel,* the weekly newspaper I write for on a freelance basis. I asked people there if they had heard anything about the abandoned horses, but no one had. I enjoyed my prime rib steak at the Caribou Grill, an imposing round-log building with a cathedral ceiling, but all the while, I couldn't stop thinking about those horses.

The sixty-kilometre drive home took longer than usual, the roads icy from the trace of snow that had fallen earlier. The night sky dazzled with stars, like so many jewels scattered on black velvet. It was close to eleven o'clock when I arrived home. I checked the thermometer outside the basement door: fifteen degrees Celsius below zero.

I had by this point convinced myself that the abandoned horses must have succumbed. Given the snow and dropping temperatures, given what the sledder had said, I was certain, and Monika was certain, the two horses were dead and gone. What I felt most that night was a dull sadness. But until we knew their fate with certainty, we could not stop thinking about them.

Just after midnight on December 12, and seven days after their owner left Belle and Sundance to die on Mount Renshaw, someone down in the valley made a small plea on their behalf.

Glenn Daykin is thirty-four years old, a lean man with a shaven head and tattoos on his arms. The part owner of Spin Drift Power Sports, he has been fixing machines since he was fourteen years old and has lived most of his life in small-town British Columbia. His shop on 2nd Avenue, fronted by turquoise steel siding, is chock full of snowmobiles, four-wheelers, helmets and all the other accoutrements you would expect in a place that rents and repairs machines that scoot over land or snow. The air in the shop is redolent of hard plastic and motor oil, and the gleaming snow machines look much bigger and more powerful up close.

Glenn had been in the shop one day in late November when several sledders came in with some odd news.

"You're not going to believe what we saw up on Mount Renshaw," one told him. And, at first, Glenn didn't believe them. His initial reaction was stupefaction. Glenn grew up on a farm, and while machines are his bread and butter, he knows horses, too. When he asked around, he was told that a local outfitter had the situation well in hand. But when sledders kept returning to his shop with news of more sightings and when the weather turned increasingly foul, he knew he had to act. In the appeal he would broadcast on the sledders' forum, Glenn reported what he had been hearing from sledders. Some dates and details were wrong: Glenn was under the impression that the man who had left the horses behind was a hunter who had gone up there in October. But some parts of Glenn's plea were spot on: he said that with the heavy snow on the mountains, the horses would be in desperate shape, that horses didn't deserve this treatment and that many people in the valley had expressed concern about them. He appealed for more information "on this sad situation."

Glenn Daykin had sent out an SOS. But with Christmas less than two weeks away, with the valley economy so distressed, with everyone so busy with shopping and all the other obligations of the holiday season, would anyone respond? Would the plight of two pack horses register on the Robson Valley radar?

∼

On Saturday, December 13, I attended another Christmas party—this one at Monika and Tim's house. Overnight, the temperature had plummeted. It was thirty degrees below zero at my place when I walked up to the highway that evening to wait for my ride. The boards on the porch groaned and cracked, the snow crunched loudly underfoot, and my nostrils pinched in the cold. At these temperatures, exposed skin is vulnerable to frostbite in as little as fifteen minutes. The trick is to dress in layers and pay special attention to protecting the extremities—head, hands and feet—where the heat loss is most acute.

I knew before I left the house, before walking outside, that it was exceptionally frosty. Sound seems to travel better in such wicked cold. The sound of the tires on the highway—cold hard rubber meeting cold hard pavement—is a noise like nothing else. And there is something about such arctic temperatures that casts a stillness over everything. As I stood by the roadway, I admired the beautiful, clear night and the star-dappled sky. A bitter wind blew, and snow drifted across the top part of the road. Glad that I had decided to wear my warm winter boots, I wrapped my scarf tighter around my neck and pulled it up over my ears. Luckily, I didn't have to wait long for my ride.

The talk of the evening was those horses up the Renshaw. Ray and Lu were there, and Ray, especially, felt terrible that the horses had been abandoned on the mountain. He wished he could have helped save them. We were torn between faint hope that the horses might endure even this cold—but then what?—and a wish that death had come to end their suffering. Neither thought offered comfort.

At the party, we all felt the same. Disconsolate, strangely bereft. Whatever the name for this loss, it had taken place too close to home.

Chapter 5

HANDGUN—OR HAY?

On the following Monday, December 15, Logan Jeck and Leif Gunster set out for Mount Renshaw on their errand of mercy to relieve an exhausted search-and-rescue crew and tow down two sleds stuck in deep snow. That was the day they made their grim discovery: two horses clinging to life in a gully above the treeline.

And now the ball set in motion by Ray Long, Reg Marek, Monika Brown and Glenn Daykin really started to roll. That evening, Ray called Monika to share the news that the abandoned horses were alive, though barely. Monika then called me.

I was in the middle of finally writing some Christmas cards. I had been putting off all the usual preparations because I just couldn't conjure up my Yuletide spirit. I usually have my house decorated the first weekend in December and, shortly after, start baking a variety of Swiss Christmas cookies, from recipes passed down from my grandmother. But I still hadn't done any baking or decorating. Normally driven and energetic, I was feeling over-worked, tired and generally sorry for myself.

"This is not going to make you feel better, what I am going to tell you," Monika said. She relayed what she knew: the two starving horses were alive and trapped in six feet of snow on Mount Renshaw, a point some forty-five kilometres from McBride and accessible only by snowmobile. Their plight seemed hopeless. News of the two horses on the mountain had triggered in several individuals an urgently felt impulse to rescue them, but still vague was who would do the rescuing, and how, and who would lead the effort—not to mention who would decide their fate: let the horses live and try to get them out or end their misery. A clock had begun to tick.

As Monika and I talked, we started to formulate some sort of plan of action. Getting up there was the first step and the major challenge. Neither of us is a sledder.

I called Logan Jeck on his cellphone to try to get information, any information, on these horses. No answer. I called two friends with snowmobiles and, again, failed to connect. The adrenalin flowing, my frustration growing, I called another friend, who suggested I call Sara Olofsson and her partner, Matt Elliott. Luckily, I immediately got Sara—someone I knew, but not well—and explained the dreadful situation.

Funny, outrageous and sharp, Sara is a lifelong horsewoman. Her first word, at the age of two, was "horse." By four, she was on her first horse. By nine, she had saved up $900 to buy her first saddle horse. I knew I could count on her. I told Sara that I was looking for someone to sled up there and see if these horses needed to be put down or if they could be helped.

Before I could finish my plea, Sara looked at Matt, as she put it, "the way only a woman can," and he agreed to go up the following day. Matt—a quiet man then thirty-one years old—also had a soft spot for animals, so Sara's sell was an easy one even though the ride was apparently difficult, especially with a passenger on board.

Sara promised me that Matt would get me there safely. "Just hang on as tight as you can, and you'll be fine," Sara told me.

Then I thought better of the plan. None of us knew precisely where the horses were or what the terrain was like. I didn't know

Matt nor how good a snowmobiler he was; I knew only that his having a passenger on board would make tricky sledding trickier. As much as I wanted to go, I worried that I would slow Matt down, so I reluctantly declined. I told him what to look for when deciding whether to keep the horses alive or not, and I underlined the risk of colic from overfeeding. "One flake of hay for each horse," I instructed him. "No more. The horses should be alert, with their heads up. If not . . ."

Sara and Matt spent the next few hours getting everything organized, and Sara—reinforcing what I had said—carefully instructed Matt on what to look for when making his difficult choice. "Look at the eyes," Sara told Matt. "You'll know. If the horses have fight, if they're standing on their own, if they want to leave when you do— those are all good signs. Pinch the skin: in two or three seconds, it should go flat again. Longer means dehydration. And, finally, check their manure. Diarrhea is not good."

Matt seemed fired up by the mission. "I don't care if no one else is going," he said. "I'm going."

Come what may, something was being done for those horses, and I took a little consolation in that.

⁓

What I hadn't known when I called Sara that day is that the name Matt Elliott gave the rescue attempt instant legitimacy. Matt is a logger and heavy equipment operator who works both in the Robson Valley and in Alberta. He studied specialty mechanics in college and can operate heavy equipment of all kinds—from complicated machines such as dangle-head processors to skidders, cats and wheel loaders.

More important, he is—here where the snowmobile is a kingpin in the local economy—a champion sledder. He started sledding when he was fifteen years old. A dirt-bike accident had broken both legs above the ankle and put him in a wheelchair for six months. Matt remembers how frightened he was that he would never escape that chair. "I would have sold my soul to walk," he says. It drove the teenager crazy that he couldn't ski that winter, but when a friend took him out on a snowmobile, young Matt was immediately hooked. And then came the competitions.

"I did okay a few times" is how he puts it. In fact, he has twice, in 2002 and 2003, won the hill-climbing championship at Jackson Hole, Wyoming—the most famous snowmobile competition in the world. These invitation-only contests draw up to three hundred sledders vying for trophies. Winners end up with big-name sponsors and are celebrated on spectacular videos that feature daring climbs, sharp turns and spraying snow from very muscular machines.

Four-year-old boys on the streets of McBride see Matt as a hero and fashion mogul. They love his Arctic Cat jacket and tricked-out lifted diesel truck. The kids sheepishly say hi to him on the sidewalk. For these children, Matt has star quality.

A natural competitor, Matt hates losing. And when the naysayers said that getting two horses off Mount Renshaw in mid-winter couldn't be done, people like Matt saw it as a challenge to be overcome in his own backyard.

While Matt prepared for the next day, Monika called me to relay what she had learned from Leif—that the horses' condition was, as he put it, "bad enough to make a person cry. Those two horses looked like really skinny Holstein cows, with their hipbones sticking out and all the ribs showing."

Leif said the mare and gelding appeared very weak and that had he carried a gun with him, he wouldn't have hesitated to end their misery. But by the time he got down to the valley, it was getting dark and temperatures were dropping again, so it would have been too dangerous to go back up. Leif told Monika that after a great many phone calls it had been decided that he and several others— Logan, his older sister, Toni and Matt—would return to the mountaintop the following day to assess the situation further. Monika advised him to be careful about feeding the horses hay without giving them water, as they might colic.

~

On the morning of Tuesday, December 16, a single party of three men and one woman on three snowmobiles—Logan with Toni doubled up on one sled and Matt and Leif each driving their own machines—went up Mount Renshaw to the horses. The day was cold and overcast, and the mountain looked to be nearly devoid of sledders.

The four had brought a handgun and a bale of hay, attached by bungee cords to one of the sleds. By mid-morning, they reached the horses. Matt, seeing them for the first time, was struck by the close confines of their enclosure—about the dimensions of a dining room table, he thought to himself. The two sorry horses just stared blankly at the group. The would-be rescuers found themselves returning the horses' dull stares. Only Matt had no experience of horses; the other three were horse people, and they simply assumed that a hunter or outfitter had lost the horses, maybe after they were spooked by the scent of bear or cougar. When that happened, it often took days to find a frightened horse in the dense forest or vast alpine. Some horses were never found.

After examining the horses more closely, the party of four agreed that despite the sad state of the creatures, there was a glimmer in their eyes. But this was ultimately Toni's call; she had the most experience. Having worked for outfitters, Toni had seen horses starve and die on the trail before. She recognized the look of imminent death. When nothing you could do was going to help them, the light in a horse's eyes would dim, and you would have to put him down. The young woman didn't hesitate; she cut the twine with her jackknife and broke open the bale of hay. Belle and Sundance weren't ready to give up. As soon as she'd gotten off the sled, Toni had seen that they still had life in their eyes. Hers was an easy decision—and a relief. She fed each horse a flake of hay (each bale "flakes" differently; a flake may be two to six inches wide and weigh three to five pounds). Toni then used a hoof pick to remove the snow and ice that had balled up under their shoes.

But the foursome still had to find a way to get the animals off the mountain. While Toni stayed with the horses, the three men, using the small collapsible avalanche shovels that sledders carry in their backpacks, started digging a deep, narrow trench—maybe a hundred feet long—from the horses' snowy prison down a steep hill and into the trees. The incredibly deep snow and the tiny shovels prolonged the job and offered the rescuers their first hint that the task at hand might prove, at worst, impossible, and, at best, a monumental challenge. Eventually, the shovellers got to the desired spot, and there the three men created a new pad for the horses, sheltered from the wind by conifers. Before heading back down to the valley, Toni fed each horse another flake of hay, a meal to sustain them as night fell.

Belle and Sundance had grown thick fur in the fall as a defence against the cold, but it takes more than fur to keep a horse warm. Horses can stand temperatures of even minus forty degrees Celsius, but to do so, they must have food. It's their fuel, their lifeline in bitter cold. Horses digest hay or grass by a fermentation process that releases heat. But these two horses had had no food and therefore had produced no heat. And the more Belle and Sundance had felt hunger, the more they'd felt the cold. They'd had no water either, and while eating snow would have provided fluid, it also would have lowered their core temperatures.

The deep snow had acted both as an ally for the two horses and as a foe. It had helped keep predators away, but as exhaustion set in and standing taxed their strength, the horses were forced to lie in the snow. Belle, in particular, had begun to lose huge sections of the fur on her sides and haunches, fur that had offered her at least some protection from the cold.

A thin, wet horse is a cold horse; worse, these horses were unable to move to generate heat. But even a thin, cold, immobilized horse can survive in winter if there's hay. If Belle and Sundance were to survive a bit longer, if this rescue had any chance, they would need hay. Lots and lots of hay.

*The first short trench that rescuers dug to get the horses
down from the alpine to their sheltered snow pad.*

~

While all this was happening up on the mountain, I was at home pacing. Armed with bits of information acquired from Monika—that the owner of the two horses was a lawyer from Edmonton named Frank and that he had had a motor vehicle accident somewhere near Mount Robson on his way home in December—I called the RCMP in Valemount, where the mishap would have taken place. But the officer on duty was close-mouthed.

"Can you look into it and, if you find out the person's name, call the SPCA in Prince George and let them know?" I pleaded with him. "This person abandoned two horses in the Renshaw area last fall, and the horses were found in that area yesterday. We are trying to locate the owner so he can help us get them out."

The officer eventually agreed, and I gave him the number of Debbie Goodine, an animal protection officer with the Society for the Prevention of Cruelty to Animals in Prince George—a two-hour drive but the closest location to McBride.

I then called the RCMP in McBride and talked to the clerk, Lorrie Lewis, who was appalled to learn that the horses were still up on the mountain. She told me that back in September, their owner had informed her that he had left his two pack horses up by the Renshaw cabin because they were too tired to walk all the

Belle (left) and Sundance, as they were found,
pictured here with rescuer Spencer Froese.

way out of the backcountry after he'd extricated them from the bog. The man had said he'd return for them on his next days off, and Lorrie, in turn, had given him the names of local outfitters who could help him. Having heard nothing more from the horses' owner, Lorrie had assumed that he'd successfully retrieved the animals. The RCMP clerk now promised to search the files for his name and, if successful, contact the SPCA in Prince George.

All day, my thoughts drifted. Were the horses still alive? Or had Matt put them down by now? I was almost hoping he had so they wouldn't have to suffer one more minute. Besides, at this point, I couldn't even imagine how we would possibly manage to get those two horses down the mountain.

By mid-afternoon, I still hadn't heard from the sledders. What was taking them so long? Had something gone wrong? Finally, I received an email from Joette Starchuck, another horse lover and McBride resident: Bob Elliott, Matt's dad, had just told her that Matt had found the horses. "He left a bale of hay, water and molasses. Apparently going back tomorrow . . ."

I felt a bit better at hearing this news, but I wanted specifics. I needed to talk to Matt. When I finally reached him, he told me that the horses were very skinny, that one had lost hair on both sides, but that they seemed alert and had wanted to follow the sledders out when they'd left in the late afternoon. That was, for me and for many who were told of it, a wrenching detail but yet more proof that the horses' spirits were not yet broken by cold and hunger. They wanted off the mountain, and they knew that these humans and their machines offered a possible way out.

Matt and the others planned to return the following day to feed the horses once more, to start digging a trail and, they hoped, to get the horses to the logging road below. Matt, for one, felt very upbeat about it all and didn't think it would take that long to get the horses to safety. Maybe a few days. At first, I felt elated by this news. Then the doubts came. What about all that snow? Were the horses that close to the logging road?

I really wanted to go up there and help and, of course, to see the horses for myself rather than rely on second-hand information. Work got in the way. This was Tuesday; the earliest I could go was Thursday, and Matt couldn't guarantee me a spot on his sled. It would depend on how many others were making the trip.

But if I couldn't go, I could at least marshal others. I called Lisa Levasseur. She once worked for a big Arabian horse farm in California called Baywood Park, where she rose through the ranks, from groom to trainer to manager of shows and sales. Various injuries—car accidents and "horse wrecks," as riders call calamitous falls—precluded her from riding anymore, but love for horses still burned inside her. I knew that she owned eighteen horses, all retired from active duty, and that she had taken in starving horses in the past.

More important, Lisa's father's Terracana Ranch Resort was frequented by sledders. I was looking for manpower, sledders and diggers, and I was hoping that Lisa could muster some.

We discussed various options for liberating the horses. We talked about airlifting them out to the cabin close by, and from there getting them into a horse trailer pulled behind the groomer on the snowmobile trail. Lisa then called Sara and Matt to discuss the idea further, and Sara called the groomer to run the idea past him. I also talked to Monika and Reg extensively that evening while looking at maps on Google Earth, trying to figure out exactly where on that impossibly huge mountain those horses stood. Surely half the phone lines in the Robson Valley were hosting conversations about those horses that night.

Pure instinct had kicked in. We didn't stop to think about how this rescue attempt might unfold or how much time it would require or what the odds were of succeeding. Many people in the valley own animals and feel compassion for them. Since so many of us also live perilously close to the highway or rail line, finding an animal in need is a common occurrence in this part of the world. It may be that the pioneer spirit still prevails in this remote valley. Or that in a small town, a common cause is more keenly felt. On big city freeways, commuters pass stranded drivers all the time, knowing that formal help (a police car, a tow truck) will soon arrive. But on a country road, the dispatching of formal help takes longer, so we stop for stricken travellers. Odds are that in the broken-down car sits someone you know, a neighbour or friend or someone who knows a neighbour or friend. In the Robson Valley, it isn't six degrees of separation. One or two is more like it.

My sleep that night was shallow and restless. I dreamt of the two horses standing in a narrow, deep hole, surrounded by high walls of snow—a prison that resembled a small yet deep swimming pool, made of snow and ice. In my dream, I stood alone atop one of the walls, looking down on the two pathetic-looking creatures and feeling sad, disillusioned and confounded by their predicament. While I was puzzling over how to get them out, I threw hay down to the starving animals. Then in the distance, far away, I heard the drone of snowmobiles. Eventually, in my dream, Matt drove to the lip of the would-be grave. "We'll get them out of there," he said confidently. Then I woke up.

Chapter 6

THE DIGGING STARTS

At 10 a.m. on Wednesday, December 17, eight volunteers met in the Renshaw parking lot. They drained the last bit of coffee from their Thermoses before unloading their sleds from their truck beds and heading up the mountain. Temperatures had dipped to minus twenty-four Celsius the night before, and the bright sun, though welcoming, was doing little to warm things up.

The first day of digging drew Dave Jeck (Logan's dad), Matt Elliott and Stuart MacMaster (Dave's brother-in-law)—the three stalwarts as I later came to call them for all the time they spent on the mountain—plus Dean Schreiber, who put in almost as many days as the stalwarts, along with Leif Gunster, Logan Jeck, another local man named Anthony Pepper and Toni Jeck. The mood was buoyant in some quarters. Matt, especially, felt confident that with all this help, the horses would be off the mountain by the end of the day.

The eight volunteers chatted about the weather and how they had dressed against the cold—as they would if they were going sledding for the day. They had their avalanche shovels, as they always did, but no other gear. Casting a glance up the mountain, Dave wondered what awaited them and what gear they'd have to bring the next day.

The plan was to make a plan, but only after seeing for themselves the lay of the land. Dave wondered how deep the snow was, whether it would be loose or packed. Maybe there would be no next day. Like Matt, Dave hoped they could just walk the horses out and down the mountain.

The ride up to the horses was long, almost an hour long, in bone-chilling cold. Wind chill from flying along on those snow machines just added more menace to the cold, still air.

When Dave Jeck finally glimpsed those two horses on the

mountain, just shy of 11 a.m., his heart went out to them. *Wow!* he thought. *They're still alive!* To see them standing there in all that snow made him angry. If you can't get horses out and if you can't put them down yourself, he said to himself, arrange for someone else to do it. No use dwelling on that now.

Belle and Sundance rewarded the eight rescuers for their arduous trek up the mountain with a whinny—accompanied by a beseeching look. This was a muted yet brave greeting. Something to build on.

After each horse was fed a flake of hay from the bale brought up the day before, Dave quickly determined that the first job to be done was to get the front shoes off those horses. Toni had used a hoof pick the day before to clean their feet of snow and ice, but Dave saw that the snow and ice had once more balled up under their shoes, making standing more difficult. So he pulled the shoes off and cleaned the horses' hooves.

Next, the group built a fire. The horses—thanks to the efforts of diggers the day before—were parked in their new snowy enclosure in the woods and out of the worst of the wind. Four feet away, the fire enabled the melting of snow for water and gave rescuers at least a semblance of warmth.

The volunteers gathered around the fire for a strategy session. Their first thought was that they could simply stamp their feet, pack down the snow as hard as they could and walk down the

*A campfire was built each day, to melt snow to water
the horses and to warm the hands of rescuers.*

mountain to the logging road, with the horses following. So the eight rescuers struck a comic pose, driving their boots into the snow—as if in anger. The stompers imagined that they had created the beginnings of a path out, and Dave led one horse, with Toni to follow with another. They would do this, they thought, fifty yards at a time with one destination in mind: the logging road.

But as skinny as they were, the horses still weighed seven to nine hundred pounds each, and the lead horse, the gelding, didn't make two steps before he was buried up to his shoulders in snow. The mare, following, had a somewhat easier time plowing through the trail he had broken. But the snow was far deeper than the rescuers had imagined, and the cold made compacting the snow almost impossible. Turning the gelding around and getting him back to the snowy enclosure was not too difficult, and the two horses certainly co-operated, doing their best to help. But the rescuers now issued a collective "Uh-oh. So much for that plan."

Back at the fire, the diggers looked ahead. Cold, they knew, was the enemy, but so was time. What shape would the next day take, and the one after that? How many days of digging were called for? Good questions, and no one had any answers.

$\sim$

It was decided that a reasonable target for leaving the parking lot every day was 10 a.m. The sledders would get to Belle and Sundance shortly before 11 a.m. By 4 p.m., all eight rescuers knew, it started to get dark on the mountain in winter, so they would have to leave the horses by 3 p.m. A four-hour window. No, less. Diggers would have to stop periodically to rest or eat or drink fluids, and a wood fire would have to be built and maintained so hands and feet could be warmed and snow melted for the horses to drink.

After some discussion, the group decided that the only way to get the horses out was to dig a deep trench, almost to the ground, all the way down to the logging road. Once on that wide, groomed road, they figured, they could walk the horses the almost thirty kilometres to the parking lot and, from there, trailer them out.

The trench would have to start a few feet below the horses so they wouldn't be tempted to exit their snow pen and try to follow the volunteer brigade down the trail after each day of digging. The trench's dimensions would need to be at least three feet wide and six feet deep. Precise length, to be determined. Precise path and angle down the mountain, to be determined.

Those in the group experienced with horses knew that horses are claustrophobic and that the trench solution was risky. But until and unless some other option presented itself, this, they believed, offered the only way out for Belle and Sundance.

Matt Elliott, one of the core people involved in the rescue effort, spent
six days digging what came to be known as "the tunnel to freedom."

Wearing his snowshoes, Dave set out to find a feasible route
from the horses' present location to the logging road, but he
quickly discovered that a direct line down entailed a steep descent
and too many gullies. *Tomorrow*, he thought, *I'll scout for a better
route*. Meanwhile, the diggers worked in the general direction of
the logging road.

After a little experimenting, the shovellers soon developed a

simple but efficient system: split up and spread out. The first shovellers dug down in the snow several feet, then moved ahead. The
next two took the trail down another foot or two, then moved
ahead, and so on. For a time, it looked as if the rescuers were building a set of snow stairs down the mountain, but eventually, the
required depth was reached, and on it went. Spreading out also
offered a psychological advantage: at the end of the day, each dig-
ger felt part of a team that had dug a hundred metres of trench.

Better yet, some team members were old friends. Dave Jeck,
Matt Elliott and Stu MacMaster were sledding pals who had jour-
neyed up the mountain together many times and gotten into—
and out of—some jams on occasion. The core of Team Belle &
Sundance comprised three men who knew, liked and trusted each
other, and that bond held true on the mountain.

~

Dave Jeck quickly emerged as a leader of the team. Dave is a fifty-
two-year-old cowboy who looks as though he just stepped off a
billboard where he had posed as the Marlboro Man. Tall and slim
with greying hair and moustache, Dave is the kind of quietly confident, easygoing man people instinctively trust, and he proved a
perfect choice to head up the rescue effort.

"My brother Gord and I started going up in the hills after high school," he told me. "For twenty-five years, we ran Jeck Brothers Outfitters in the McBride area. We once spent a hundred and twenty days in the Yukon, way back in the mountains, working for an outfitter there." The brothers sold their business in 2004, but Dave still has eight horses at home.

Dave took a matter-of-fact approach to the idea of getting horses off a mountaintop. He would not classify himself as a horse lover. A pragmatist, more like it. "I had to shoot a crippled horse once," he told me. "I've had horses get old and then they get a stroke and you have to shoot them. I don't cry over them. I'm more realistic. I like horses and I look after them, but I'm not an extremist. I won't cry if one dies. People can get radical when it comes to horses."

Lana, Dave's wife, is fond of telling people that once Dave sets his mind on something, "he's like a dog with a bone." After seeing the horses up on Mount Renshaw, he simply said to himself, "I'm getting those horses out of there. They need help." Dave Jeck felt certain that he and a few good men could dig those horses out.

As for the cold, he's almost cavalier. "I log in the winter. You can't stand around," he jokes. "You'll freeze."

The first thing Dave had done after Logan had told him about the two horses stuck on the mountain was call his brother-in-law, Stu MacMaster. "Of course I'll come," Stu had said. Dave later

Stuart MacMaster and Dave Jeck warm up by the campfire.

called Lester Blouin, who had worked for ten years as a hunting guide for Jeck Brothers. Lester had been out of town, but when he got back, he said pretty much the same thing. "Count me in."

A powerfully built man with a weathered face and blue eyes, Lester was born a hundred and fifty years too late. He uses Percherons (he has ten) to seed his one hundred and thirty-five acres in the spring, to cut his hay through summer and fall and to log in the winter. He admits that machines are quicker, but he enjoys walking behind his towering black horses as they work, and he likes being able to grow hay as fuel.

Lester loves horses, but that alone didn't explain why he signed on in a heartbeat to the Belle and Sundance assignment. In our spectacularly beautiful but isolated community (Vancouver is a nine-hour drive to the southwest, Edmonton is six hours to the east), helping one another is instinctive and natural. "If we see smoke," Lester once told a visitor from away, "we call and we go there. In the city, it might take them a while to come together. Here you don't think about it. You just go."

Stuart MacMaster, like Dave, is accustomed to working in minus-thirty-degree cold. A logger all his life, Stu stays lean and fit, not by visiting the gym or jogging but by labouring over big timber with chainsaws and axes.

So as the crew turned to digging, Stuart relaxed. Although the shovelling was hard work, he was used to that. The hardest part for Stu had been the ride up the mountain and the ride down. An avid sledder, Stuart often drove his red and black Arctic Cat up and down that mountain, and he had all the gear—including black snowmobile pants, a kind of high-bib coverall meant to keep a person warm on a mountain—but that day's cold was so harsh, the coverall wasn't doing the job. However, once he got moving

In the bowl below Mount Renshaw, near the horses' snowy prison.

and kept moving, kept digging, he was fine. *Head down, ass up and shovel snow*, Stuart thought as he dug.

Motivation never posed an issue for Stu. When Dave Jeck described the situation to him, Stuart just signed on. It wasn't necessarily about horses. It was about helping, about doing what was required because the alternative was intolerable. "It's no big deal," he said. "It's what we do here. Someone had to do something."

Stu had worked with horses a bit, though he wouldn't dare call himself a horseman. He has a dog, a heeler-shepherd, and a sensitivity for animals. And besides, he wasn't working at the time. Case closed.

~

While the diggers dug, Belle and Sundance ate their hay. At the end of that first day of digging, Stu thought he could see a change in the horses. They looked a tad brighter, a little more interested in things.

Riding down that night, the team endured an hour of blistering cold and cutting wind. But for Stuart MacMaster, it was one more trip through God's country. As they sped down the mountain, he felt what he often felt up here—a powerful blend of gratitude and awe. Stuart was thinking three things:

We live in beauty.
This is the best valley in the world.
And I do not take it for granted.

Chapter 7
"HI GUYS"

On Thursday, December 18, it was my turn, finally, to go up the mountain. I didn't sleep much the previous night. Nervous and excited, I couldn't wait to see the horses for myself. By morning, Matt had said the evening before, he would know who was going up the mountain and whether he could take me. He'd told me that if he was forced to choose between me and a big, strong man, he would take the man, who most likely would make the better shoveller.

"No offence," he'd said.

"I can shovel," I'd countered. "I shovel every day at home, horse manure and snow." I was determined to prove myself, given the opportunity.

I phoned Matt at 8.30 a.m. sharp, as he had instructed me. First the line was busy, then there was no answer. I feared he had left without me.

∽

The idea of the horses being up there, stranded in the snow and the cold, was weighing more heavily on me than I had at first thought.

"Don't get consumed by all this," my husband, Marc, kept telling me, even though he feels the same compassion for animals that I do. A tall, slim, olive-skinned man, he feels most at home in cowboy boots and a Stetson, with a guitar on his lap and a cowboy song on his lips.

Marc himself was angry about the horses having been abandoned in the mountains. "The owner just walked away. I wouldn't have done it, and I'm a poor man," he said later.

I met Marc through a co-worker in Hinton, Alberta, where I wrote for a newspaper. Marc was working in nearby Jasper for Parks Canada's highways department. We married in 2002 under the birch tree I pass every day en route to our horse pasture. I was born a Capricorn, and people born under that sign are notoriously stubborn and persistent, head-through-the-wall persistent. Marc is a Gemini, a lone wolf with two personalities. The one is very quiet, the other quite social. He and I had just clicked.

Marc had grown up in Parry Sound, in central Ontario, where he experienced an attraction to animals as strong as my own. He would clean box stalls just so he could ride a horse. Marc had come west as a young man and found work tar-roofing in Edmonton and later with the Canadian National Railway. Once he had seen Banff, he was hooked on living in the mountains. Marc is a self-taught rider, but he is also fearless, and most horses under him take comfort in that.

Like many in the Robson Valley, Marc has to go elsewhere for work, commuting back home on weekends and days off. In winter, he drives a snowplow in Jasper National Park. In summer, he drives a truck hauling gravel, fixes roads and signs and, during forest fires, transports chainsaws, hoses and fuel to fire bases. Marc is gone from the ranch four to five days every week, longer if there are fires. He sleeps in a tin-can camper during his workweek, then comes home to unending rounds of farm chores.

I was grateful that he was there on that stressful Thursday morning as I fretted over whether Matt had or had not left for Mount Renshaw without me. Marc suggested I call Tony Parisi, an outfitter and snowmobile guide who lives in Valemount. I reached Tony right away and, after explaining the circumstances, asked him if he could take me up the mountain.

But Tony had blown his sled's engine, and his truck had broken down, too. "I'm sorry, Birgit," he said. "But if Matt said he was going to take you, he will." (Just a note on my name: my Canadian friends pronounce it Ber-geet, while in Europe the stress is on the first syllable, as in Beer-git.)

Tony knows Matt very well, so his words offered me some assurance. Still, I could not make sense of Matt's line being busy one minute and going unanswered the next. I ended my call with Tony by asking him to spread the word that we needed sledders to help us shovel.

Finally, just before 9 a.m., the phone rang. It was Matt.

"So, do you still want to go?"

"You bet," I said.

"We're meeting at the Renshaw parking lot at ten."

I had had no breakfast yet, but I couldn't eat anyway. My stomach was in knots.

I raced to get ready. Getting dressed for the mountain is no simple matter. The rule is to dress in layers, starting with several pairs of socks, long underwear, then fleece pants, a turtleneck and two fleece sweaters, a neck warmer, a fleece vest, jogging pants and insulated bib coveralls. Then I gathered up my toque, two balaclavas, several pairs of gloves and mitts, Sorel winter boots, ski goggles and my thick oilskin coat. I also got my snowshoes ready, just in case.

Finally, I double-checked the contents of my backpack: my camera, cellphone, salt and electrolytes for the horses, a syringe to make an electrolyte drench (a mix of powdered electrolytes and water), a notebook, a pen and a bottle of water, as well as a lunch, including some of my favourite Christmas cookies. I had finally gotten around to making two kinds.

I'd learned that Tim and Monika were coming as well—a relief since I wasn't certain that anyone else I knew would be there. Monika asked me to bring some warm gear for her—she didn't own the heavy-duty winter clothing required for a mountain-top—so I packed another pair of Sorel boots, Marc's thick, long army coat (which he swears you could sleep in comfortably during forty-below weather), his lined winter overalls and an extra pair of goggles.

From McBride, it's almost twenty kilometres to the parking lot. Just before the bridge over the Fraser River, I turned off the high-way and followed Mountainview Road, which runs parallel to the river before heading northwest alongside the Rocky Mountains for a good long stretch. As I turned into the lot, a few sledders were busy unloading their machines. When I asked if they were here for the horse rescue, they looked amused and shook their heads no.

The cold had bite, and the wind blowing snow across the wide-open field from the east made that bite even fiercer. I walked back to my truck and sat inside. It was too frigid to stand around in that nasty wind.

Finally, someone who was actually part of the horse rescue showed up. Spencer Froese and Joey Rich were the first ones, and I was happy to see their familiar faces. Spencer's mother, Irene, and his sister Robertta had taken riding lessons from me in the past. They lived just southeast of town on a grain farm and also raised buffalo. Then Lester Blouin arrived, with a borrowed snowmobile and his skimmer—an eight-by-three-foot heavy plastic sled that farmers use to pull newborn calves from the field to shelter. The crew planned to load the skimmer with all the gear needed to get the rescue operation rolling.

Matt, whom I had never met in person, arrived next. He and I had been talking for several days on the phone, and it was nice, finally, to put a face to the voice. Dave Jeck followed with his daughter Toni, who nodded in my direction.

Toni was born into a horse family and has worked in northern British Columbia as a wrangler; she and I have a love of horses in common, but neither of us has warmed to the other. People who are passionate about horses do not always see eye to eye. I once read a vet's theory on why the horse world is marked by so much jealousy and antagonism: he observed that riding a horse is about a human controlling an animal who may weigh six or seven times what the human does, so a room full of horse people is sometimes a room full of controllers. However, I thought to myself, this was a time for Toni and me to put our differences aside.

Leif showed up shortly afterward. I met Leif eight years ago when Marc and I first moved to the valley and bought hay from his parents, whose farm is halfway between Dunster and McBride. I hadn't seen him since he was a young teenager; he was now a grown man. I would never have recognized him.

I felt encouraged by this assemblage of people. Lester wasn't in the best of health, but he had come. And so had all these others. I was impatient to start, and feeling good about our prospects.

We loaded Lester's skimmer with the following: two winter horse blankets (they were lined and buckled at the belly so they'd fit snugly over a horse's torso), two square bales of hay, several shovels and a roll of road carpet. Someone had suggested we try to walk the horses out on it. Until ruled out, all options remained on the table. More hay and shovels were loaded onto the sleds and tied down with bungee cords. Leif, Spencer and Joey took off on their sleds first, with Matt and me not far behind them.

I had never been on a snowmobile before. I had driven lots of four-wheelers but usually just for short trips to feed horses or check fences. I wasn't the type of person who used such machines for pleasure. To me, they existed for a practical reason—to make my job easier. So being a passenger on a snowmobile took some getting used to. I slid on the cold and slippery plastic seat and found it difficult to hang on at the beginning. It ultimately occurred to me that the seat wasn't meant to hold two people. Matt was such an expert driver, though, that I was never worried or frightened. Instead, I enjoyed the scenery. The ride through the narrow valley, along the frozen Blackwater River, was absolutely breathtaking. The deep blue of the mountain sky, the pristine white of the snow and the gleaming silver of the ice on the branches and treetops are some of the brightest and purest colours in creation.

"Have you never been up here before?" Matt asked. He seemed shocked when I said no.

Matt sits a snowmobile the way I sit a horse. We each look comfortable and completely at home on our respective mounts. For Matt, a sled offers adrenalin-fuelled thrills, the chance to cover ground that would take weeks by foot or horseback, and views of peaks and valleys that photographs and video can never really capture. Seeing them with my own eyes, I understood for the first time why sledders came up here in such numbers.

Half an hour into the ride, the valley widened and we drove through several cut blocks—large areas that have been clear-cut by logging companies. The Rocky Mountains lay before us in all their majesty. At one point, Matt stopped and pointed toward one of the mountains. "That's where the horses are," he said.

"Way up there?" I asked. He nodded. It still seemed so far away.

About ten minutes further along, Matt guided his snowmobile off the logging road and started veering uphill. Here the horse trail led off to the left. The trail we took, to the right—the same one the horses' owner had mistakenly taken—was known by locals to be impassable in summer due to thick downfall and bog. The ascent was quite steep at times, and I had to hang on tightly to Matt to avoid sliding off the back of the snowmobile.

When we reached the Mount Renshaw warming hut, we briefly stopped and went inside. Leif sat alone in the cabin, munching on a sandwich. Matt steered me to the back window and pointed. "That's where we're headed."

We didn't rest there long. I really wanted to see the horses. Beyond the cabin, the trail was no longer groomed and the terrain was wide open. The scene struck me as unforgettably beautiful, but wild and rugged, even menacing, and the depth of snow defied belief. The average winter snowfall on the Renshaw is ten feet. To traverse the mountain with a passenger and avoid getting stuck in that depth of powdery snow, a snowmobiler has to be very skilled. And Matt is that. He instructed me to slide to the front of the snowmobile while he stood behind me, steering his sled carefully. The ride was very bumpy, and more than once my chin glanced off the handlebar. But I didn't care. I was just so exhilarated to finally be up here.

At the top of a steep hill, just below Mount Renshaw, Matt stopped again and aimed a gloved finger down toward the treeline at the bottom of the bowl. "That's where they are," he said.

I didn't know a snowmobile could go down such a precipitous slope as the one we now descended, with Matt once more at the front and me behind. I wasn't frightened, thanks to Matt, but the steep drop offered a wild adrenalin rush.

Spencer and Joey were already waiting at the spot where the horses had been found three days earlier. Matt showed me the trench that he and the other volunteers had dug so they could walk the horses down into the shelter of the trees. I could see bits and pieces of hay, remnants of the first meal the two horses had eaten in a long, long time.

I stumbled down the narrow trench surrounded by high walls of snow. How on earth, I wondered, did they get those horses to walk through this steep passageway? My mind raced. I was impatient to see the horses but, on the other hand, worried that I would be really upset by the sight that awaited me. The track was slippery, and I practically ran downhill, almost falling on top of the horses, who looked at me curiously. Both whinnied, that high-pitched hello that horses use with both humans and each other.

"Hi guys," I said to them. One by one, I stroked the horses' shoulders, ran my hands down their backs, and offered what comfort I could by touch.

They looked horrendous, with their hips and tailbones protruding, with fur and tails missing. The gelding's tail was almost completely chewed off; only the dock (the bony part of the tail from which the long hair grows) retained a little hair. The mare's tail had somewhat more hair, but she was missing huge patches on her sides and haunches, shoulders and forelegs. It looked as though someone had haphazardly and erratically clipped her, leaving her that much more vulnerable to the cold. At first, some of us blamed lice or rain scald, but we later concluded that she had suffered frostbite from reclining in the snow.

Both horses were emaciated, their backs were covered in snow and ice, and the mare was shivering. They looked pathetic, but I was pleasantly surprised—even taken aback—by how alert they were. Their eyes were clear, their ears were up, and they were curious about me. All signs pointed to the same conclusion: they wanted to live. I now understood why the group had decided not to shoot them but, instead, to give them a fighting chance.

Following Dave Jeck's instructions, I fed each horse a flake of hay; they ate it eagerly. Before going up on the mountain, I had

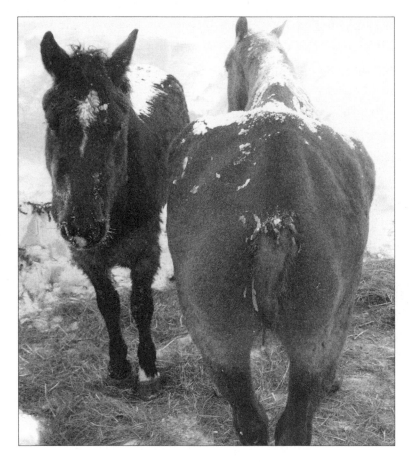

When Belle (left) and Sundance were discovered, Belle was missing huge patches of hair, and the horses had gnawed each other's tails in an attempt to avoid starvation.

heard about a plan to feed alfalfa cubes to the horses. Monika had told me this, but she had had many conversations about the stranded pair and couldn't recall who had told her.

"What?" I'd said. "They're going to kill them!"

I had no experience with rescuing starving horses, but I knew this much: alfalfa is far too rich a food for weak horses. The day before, I had contacted Rick Maitlin, part of the Rescue 100 Foundation based in Alberta, a group that had rescued a hundred starving Arabian horses in the spring of 2008. I had particular questions about salt and electrolytes.

"I agree with you," Rick had written in an email. "No cubes! Grass hay is by far the best, but if not available something with limited alfalfa. A salt/mineral block is okay providing they have water to drink. Electrolytes are a good idea as well, but again they should have water for this. Their electrolyte level is probably way off. NO OATS!"

I had worried a little that a tense standoff might have developed on the mountain if anyone had notions of feeding the horses alfalfa cubes, but it turned out no such plans existed; we all agreed on how to feed the horses. The alfalfa cubes rumour had been just that—a rumour. One of many.

It was important that the horses continue receiving the same amount of food they'd been fed thus far. Dave suggested this

Birgit Stutz (left), sitting on Stuart MacMaster's snowmobile, and
Leif Gunster bring hay bales to the horses.

routine: I feed the horses the instant I got there each morning
and just before I left each afternoon so we could spread out the
horses' two feedings as much as possible. This made perfect sense,
and it's what I do with my own horses. Feeding the horses, watering them, ensuring they were fed according to a strict protocol—
this became my job, one I felt very comfortable doing.

Spencer joined me in the snow pen and began working on the

mare's urine-encrusted tail, or at least its remnant. Frozen urine clung to her tail hair in chunks of pale yellow ice. With the little saw on his Swiss Army knife, Spencer began cutting while I held the tail away from the mare's body and tried to separate the hair to be cut from that to be saved.

"Is my cheek red?" Spencer asked me at one point, holding his cheek with one hand.

His cheek was beet red and obviously causing him pain. We later learned that he had suffered severe frostbite. He wasn't the only one. Dean Schreiber—a neighbour of Dave Jeck who would spend four days shovelling on the mountain—would also suffer frostbite on his face and hands, and Leif would get touched by it, too. They were "lit up," as we say—touched by frost.

With only two avalanche shovels, Spencer and I then started digging the trench, as well as we could, a few feet below the horses' little snow fort. The going was painfully slow, but at least the activity kept us warm.

Soon after, we heard snowmobiles in the distance, and in due time the rest of that day's digging crew—Dave Jeck, Toni Jeck, Monika and Tim Brown, Leif Gunster and Lester Blouin—came barrelling down the hill between the trees and right up to the horses. The horses didn't spook or even stir and barely looked up from their hay. Belle and Sundance, it seemed, had already started

Sundance's mane was covered in icicles, earning him the nickname "Reggae."

to connect the sound and sight of snowmobiles with meal time. The two horses were friendlier now than they'd been on that first day when Matt and the others had approached them, more pushy and feeling like themselves, butting the rescuers with their heads.

At this point, we didn't know the horses' names. Monika started calling the gelding Hippie because the ice in his mane made her think of beads. Tim then came up with Reggae, which Monika liked better. The Browns called the mare—what else—Renshaw. So Reggae and Renshaw they became.

We unloaded the sleds and formed small teams to try to put the blankets on the horses. Though the mare continued to shiver, she nevertheless kept moving away from us—probably because she had never had a blanket on before. Sundance quietly munched his hay while we worked around him, suggesting one of three explanations: he knew about blankets, didn't know about blankets but was too weak to object or was old enough to know better than to object in any case.

I asked Monika to wrap her arms around Belle's neck so I could lay the winter blanket on the mare, who finally co-operated. The blanket was a bit too big for her, so Lester pulled some baler twine from his pocket and tied it around the front closure to make the blanket fit more snugly. Belle stopped shivering pretty quickly; the hay had begun generating some heat, and the blanket was keeping it in.

By then it was just past noon, so I quickly ate my sandwich and cookies, then grabbed my snow shovel and went back to digging. Meanwhile, some of the crew gathered dry branches and started a fire. Dave had brought a metal bucket, and the men packed it with snow and hung it on a big branch over the fire so we could water the horses. The slow, tedious process reminded me just how much snow must melt to produce one litre of water. Ten to twelve inches

Sundance and Belle are warm and cozy with their fresh hay and winter blankets.

of snow in a pail, once melted, might net one inch of water.

We continued to use the "stairway" system that Dave and the others had developed. This method worked really well, for it meant that shorter people, such as Monika and me, didn't have to throw snow over our heads and off to the side.

While we dug, Dave strapped on his snowshoes and walked a line to signal the path for the long trench—from the horses' pen to the groomed snowmobile trail below. At first, he figured the distance we had to shovel was about one and a half kilometres, then he recalculated and judged that one kilometre was more like it. Dave was looking for a route alongside the hill, not a direct line but one with a gentler slope. He also planned it so we'd have only one creek to cross, in a small gully just before the trench met the snowmobile trail.

It felt a lot warmer up on the mountain than it had down at the parking lot, and we were thankfully spared any wind. The sun shone with no cloud in sight, and the spellbinding view of the snow-covered mountains in the distance took me out of the serious business at hand and into a little reverie; I was taken back to my childhood skiing vacations in Switzerland. I even doffed my coat. At the end of the day, though, the back of my fleece vest was coated in ice and snow from brushing against the sides of the narrow tunnel as I shovelled, and when the sun started to dip below the Cariboo Mountains across the valley, the cold quickly regained its sharp edge.

Apart from short breaks to catch our breath and straighten our backs, drink water and grab a few bites to eat, we had shovelled for three hours.

Dave had suggested moving the horses down into the newly dug part of the trench every day and creating a new pen each time. Had a storm moved in or the wind picked up, our hard-won trench would have been buried. However, by making new pens every day, the horses would be that much closer to the snowmobile trail and our digging efforts wouldn't be wasted—no matter what the weather brought. We had all agreed on this plan, but by the end of the day, after giving the matter more thought, we all decided against it. The whole area was heavily treed and steep, meaning that getting to the horses on snowmobiles and bringing in hay would have become even more difficult.

If Belle and Sundance were to get off the mountain then, two things had to occur: the horses would have to stay put in that first pen, and the mountain weather would have to co-operate. The first was easily done; the second would require an enormous helping of good luck.

Before heading back down the mountain, I fed each horse another flake of hay and checked their blankets. The mare had drunk some water, but not the gelding, who seemed to prefer snow. At some point, one horse had kicked over the bucket with the remaining water. Because they hadn't ingested enough water, I decided against giving them electrolytes. The primary role of electrolytes is to maintain water and ionic balance in the body. But I could only safely administer electrolyte supplements—which contain minerals such as sodium, chloride and potassium—if the horses were drinking at least some water. Feeding electrolytes to a severely dehydrated horse risks transferring precious water from the circulation to the gastrointestinal tract, compounding the dehydration.

Surveying our progress, Dave said that if worse came to worst and we couldn't get the horses out, he and other sledders—Matt, Leif, Logan and Stu—would just keep coming up here regularly with hay, even if that meant doing so until spring, when we could walk them out. Although a possibility, I was not keen on that idea. Sledders might not be able to reach the horses at all if the weather turned—precisely when Belle and Sundance would need food the most to stay warm. In winter, the mountain nights are long and cold. This is why I feed my horses an extra meal at 11 p.m.—so they'll have food for heat when the temperatures are at their most bitter. With Belle and Sundance, we had to limit their intake of hay or risk colic. There was no getting around it: once the food we gave them at 4 p.m. was gone, the gelding and the mare would have to wait until 11 a.m. the next day to get more of that life-sustaining hay. I found it very difficult to leave the horses. I just wanted them off the mountain so they could be looked after properly.

And now it was time to embark on the dreaded long trip back down. The balaclavas I'd worn on the ride in were now frozen and stiff from the moisture in my breath turning to ice, and the gloves I'd worn while shovelling had likewise stiffened. I had at

Monika Brown (left) and Birgit Stutz are excited to be doing their part to rescue Belle and Sundance.

least managed to keep my other pair of gloves and a pair of mitts dry by stuffing them into my backpack. Even my goggles were frozen.

Dave asked Monika, Tim and me if we wanted to snowshoe out to the snowmobile trail. "It's easier than doubling everybody back up to the cabin," he suggested. We agreed, albeit reluctantly. Like most everyone else, I hadn't brought my snowshoes up the mountain, so we borrowed some from Dave and Spencer.

The three of us then followed Dave's snowshoe tracks from the horses toward the snowmobile trail, with Tim in front, Monika (who had never snowshoed before) in the middle, and me following. We all wiped out several times in the deep snow. The trail angled down, and every so often we would slide off Dave's tracks and catch a snowshoe before taking a tumble. The adrenalin of the day provided my fuel as I snowshoed, so I felt no fatigue. The digging had taxed one set of muscles, the snowshoeing another. Still, it was hard going.

Adding to our difficulties were the tree wells. The spreading limbs of coniferous trees prevent falling snow from reaching the base of the tree, creating deep and dangerous depressions called tree wells. Many skiers and snowboarders have died falling into them. The tree wells, of course, were lower than the tracks we followed, and it was easy to slide down into them. Parts of the "trail" coursed downhill, so we ended up sliding on our bottoms more than walking. Reaching the groomed snowmobile trail seemed to take forever but in actuality was more like twenty-five minutes.

"The snowshoeing was so exhausting," Monika said when we finally reached the snowmobile trail. "The idea of shovelling that distance seems impossible." And we would have to shovel that distance to a depth of six feet and a width of three. Like Monika, I too

Monika gets ready to snowshoe from the horses' snowy
pen to the groomed snowmobile trail.

felt frustrated and disillusioned, and harboured grave doubts that we would ever get this job done.

None of the other volunteers had arrived at the trail by the time we had. They were all in the cabin warming up while we waited for them in the cold. Since Monika and I hadn't wanted to wear our heavy coats on the hike out, we'd left them with the sledders, but now it was getting darker and colder by the minute. Finally, after what seemed like an eternity but was probably only a few minutes, we heard the drone of multiple engines and saw headlights coming around the bend and down the steep hill.

Monika, Tim and I bundled up and loaded our backpacks onto the sleds. Once we were all set, the convoy of seven snowmobiles headed down the mountain. I couldn't see a thing, and not just because it was getting dark. With my goggles frozen, I had to put full trust in Matt.

The temperature had dropped considerably since we'd left the horses. "Aren't you cold?" Matt asked me, warming his bare hands and gloves over the heat of the engine.

"I'm okay," I said. "Just my feet."

"I guess I'm the wimp today," he joked. I was grateful for the big mitts Marc had given me that morning.

By 5 p.m., when we finally arrived, pitch dark had descended and an ice-cold wind once more cut across the parking lot. Spencer's truck wouldn't start, and we spent a long time getting it going, even with booster cables.

My big old black and red truck, a 1990 Ford F-350 crew cab that I use to haul my horse trailer, whined and howled and complained but eventually came to life. I called Marc from my cellphone to let him know that we were down from the mountain, but the phone's battery was almost dead from the cold, and I worried that the cell would quit any moment. Marc had already done the chores—one less worry—and was just waiting for my call before heading to his job in Jasper, one hundred and fifty kilometres to the east. I so looked forward to relaxing and warming up at home.

~

I did get warm, but there was no relaxing. Once home, I started answering emails. A handful of people in the valley who had heard about the rescue attempt asked me for updates on the digging and how they could help. I reported on the horses' condition and told my correspondents that ten of us had dug that day. "We need help," I wrote them. "It's a huge task."

Many local people, meanwhile, had alerted the SPCA, which was trying to arrange for a veterinarian from Prince George to assess the two horses the following morning. If the vet decided that the horses should be euthanized, then this whole operation would shut down. Some of us, me included, still hoped that airlifting the horses out was an option. But the cost (more than $5,000) would be prohibitive, and the SPCA worried about wind chill and the stress on horses whose health was already compromised by exposure and prolonged malnourishment.

While we had been up on the mountain digging a trench and looking after the horses, Alison Schreiber (Dean's wife) and Sara Olofsson—unbeknownst to each other—had spent the day on the phone with the local helicopter company and posting updates on the sledders' forum.

Amazing. A few hundred people in the Robson Valley were now following the story of the horses on Mount Renshaw.

At the end of my first day of digging, I had a real sense of what we would-be rescuers faced. The first hurdle was simply getting up the mountain. Each trip required, first, driving one's car or truck to McBride from the various points in the valley where the rescuers lived, then a twenty-kilometre drive from the village up winding Mountainview Road to the Renshaw parking lot, then a thirty-kilometre trip on a snowmobile along the logging road and up the mountain in frigid temperatures made worse by wind chill, and then a traverse across the mountain high up in the alpine and a trek down two steep hills before finally reaching the horses.

The second obstacle was the forbidding cold. Sledders couldn't wear full-face helmets; they would fog up. Instead, they wore moto-cross helmets (distinguished by their exaggerated chin protectors) with the glass shield removed. The modification that Matt, Stu, Dave and the other drivers came up with was good old duct tape, put over the chin vents to keep out the cold, which seemed especially intense along the river between kilometres five and fifteen. In winter, the river acts as a sink for the cold—in the same way that frost in late fall or fog in summer will settle into low pockets. As Matt had warned on my first day, "The cold along the river will just bite you."

So there were challenges, forbidding challenges, but at least we had a plan. The team of rescuers would haul up hay every day and blankets for the horses as needed. We would melt snow in pails over campfires to water the horses. And we would do what Canadians do in winter: dig through snow with shovels and toss it high over our heads. The trench as planned would drop at about forty-five degrees and follow a trajectory from the northwest to the southeast, the same compass line that the Robson Valley, the Fraser River, the highway and the railway all followed. We also had a shovelling strategy: all currently available volunteers would continue digging near the top of the mountain. Eventually, another crew would begin digging by the snowmobile trail. If all went well, the trench diggers would meet somewhere in the middle.

∼

On Friday, December 19, Dave, Matt and Stu accompanied two SPCA constables from Kamloops, along with a veterinarian from Prince George, up to Mount Renshaw to assess the horses.

The involvement of the SPCA did not sit well with Dave Jeck. Frustrated that the digging ground to a halt while the vet and the SPCA constables were transported to the horses and back and also feeling that his horsemanship, his judgment and his knowledge—based on a lifetime around horses—wasn't being trusted, Dave believed wholeheartedly that the team of community volunteers had everything well in hand and had developed a viable plan to get these horses off the mountain. What the SPCA was doing was meddling, he thought, and a waste of precious time.

Veterinarians use a one-to-nine score to grade a horse's body condition. A score of nine indicates an extremely fat or obese horse; five is considered ideal; and a horse with a score of one is near death. Dr. Jodyne Green, the vet brought up to examine Belle and

Sundance, gave the older gelding a score of two, and the younger mare a rating of two to three. A tall, athletic young woman, the vet knew at a glance that these horses had a chance. There would be no "pulling the pin on the whole deal," as Matt had feared might happen.

All the vet's checks simply corroborated her first impression: the horses were thin but not in danger. We were to stay the course, keep doing what we were doing. Dr. Green advised against airlifting them out—for all the obvious reasons: wind chill, the added stress, the horses' poor condition.

But I knew we weren't out of the woods yet. Predators roaming the mountain might get the horses first. Wind or wind-driven snow could fill in the trench, blocking the path out. Avalanche presented another risk, especially if temperatures began to rise. That winter, twenty-six sledders died in British Columbia and Alberta, all of them buried in cascading snow. A lot could still go wrong on Mount Renshaw.

≈

While the vet was examining the horses up on the mountain, I sat at my computer trying to write stories for the *Valley Sentinel*, but I couldn't focus. I was wrestling with various unhappy scenarios when Marc called me from work and suggested alerting some of the radio stations in Edmonton and Jasper. "See if they'll put something on the air asking sledders going to McBride for the weekend to help shovel," he said.

I called CISN Country in Edmonton, which promised to air my plea, and did. I also tried to reach a radio station in Jasper but only left a message. No one returned my call.

Dave Jeck telephoned me that evening, and he wasn't pleased. "This whole thing has been blown way out of proportion," he said. He thought the operation was getting too big, with too many volunteers becoming involved. "The story of the rescue mission is all over the Internet," he complained. "Toni came across it on SnowandMud.com. It would have been better if just the core group of our family and some friends had kept going up there."

Dave had been giving some thought to adopting the horses himself—should we succeed—but as the attempted rescue of Belle and Sundance moved from a small-scale, family-and-friends operation into something larger, he changed his mind. He worried that adoption would involve the SPCA and a great deal of red tape and public scrutiny, none of which he wanted.

The Robson Valley is, in large part, populated by people who share Dave's outlook. The area served as a refuge for American draft dodgers and hippies when the Vietnam War raged, and before that, the Mennonites had come, looking to be left alone to their religion and culture. A great many people lived in the valley because they didn't like governments and bureaucracies nosing around, and here in this distant outpost, they endured less of it—though maybe not little enough to suit Dave Jeck.

I for one didn't agree with his view on keeping the rescue operation small. The more people toiling away, the quicker the path would be forged and the horses secured in a new home. "I don't think we will be able to do it by ourselves," I countered. "It's too long a trench in too much snow. And one big storm could fill it all in." I refrained, however, from telling Dave I'd contacted several radio stations with my plea for more volunteers.

In the end, we met halfway, with Dave conceding that perhaps we did need more bodies digging on the mountain. We ended on a good note, agreeing to meet in the Renshaw parking lot in the morning for another day of digging.

∾

Meanwhile, not everyone in the community was enthusiastic about what we were doing on Mount Renshaw. That evening, I read what one member of the sledders' forum had written about the lost horses:

I think the most humane thing to do in the circumstances is to quickly give them a lead injection. Take the $2,000 or $4,000 or whatever it is going to cost to get these horses out of there, and give it to the Salvation Army, Christmas Bureau, etc. to give some kids a chance this Christmas.

Barry Walline countered with this:

That would be the easy way of dealing with this situation, but here in McBride we don't just take the easy way out. . . . This small-town way of thinking has me converted. Someone or something in trouble, we go out of our way to help.

Sara posted a reply as well, but hers had bite:

Good idea, let's just shoot the horses. . . . Perhaps that is what we should do to the next rider that comes in and gets

himself or his sled stuck, and a bunch
of people donate their time and effort
and risk themselves for that endeavour
as well. We do the same to rescue a person
and even, unbelievably, a machine . . . so
why not a horse? . . . We are supposed to
be a higher life form.

When Matt heard about the "lead injection" comment, he had one thought: You wouldn't suggest that if you had seen the horses' eyes.

Chapter 8

A CHRISTMAS GIFT TO REMEMBER

My alarm roused me at dawn on Saturday, December 20. When I flicked on my bedside light, I glimpsed the first hint of just how cold it was outside—a thick coating of frost lined the inside of my bedroom window. At 6 a.m., the outdoor thermometer registered forty degrees below Celsius.

After bundling up, I headed outside to do my morning chores. I have nineteen animals on my farm (not counting the chickens), and all must be fed and watered at dawn and dusk.

Before going to the barn, I plugged in my truck. To do this, I had to unplug the power cord leading to the two heated water buckets for the horses penned by the barn. Knowing that their water would freeze in this nasty cold, I'd made the decision the night before to keep the buckets plugged in, rather than my truck. My hope was that there would be enough time that morning to warm the truck's big engine block.

My nine horses were whinnying as I prepared their feed. "You guys have it a lot better than those poor horses on the mountain, and yet you're still complaining and being impatient!" I scolded them.

When I went to start my truck, nothing happened. Keeping the horses' water buckets plugged in had been the right decision, but my old truck's battery had paid the price. I called my neighbour, Dr. Tom Vogel, our local vet, who happened to be heading the same way I was. "Can you give me a lift?" I asked him, and of course he agreed.

When Tom and I got to the Jeck farm shortly after 9 a.m., Dave informed me that he wasn't going up Mount Renshaw after all. He had an injured mare and wanted to stay home and help Tom tend to her.

"Stu is going, though," said Dave. "He can take you."

Dave then showed me the feed schedule the vet had given him the day before and asked me to ensure the horses were fed accordingly. The schedule offered mainly common sense advice—increase feed gradually, space out feedings, administer small and frequent meals if possible—and warnings that days three to seven were the most critical. That is when a starving horse being nursed back to health faces the greatest risk of dying; the right balance has to be struck between offering too little food and too much. Beyond that period, the horses could be fed grain on days eight to ten, and within ten days to two weeks, Belle and Sundance could be put on an all-you-can-eat diet.

I fashioned two cardboard signs that we intended to place next to the groomed snowmobile trail, where the trench would emerge. The signs read:

Horse Rescue. Follow trail. Please help us dig.

Soon after, Stu arrived at Dave's and we took off. Stu had filled the box of his pickup truck with square bales of hay, some of which we would take up the mountain; the rest we'd leave in the parking lot. The attendant selling sled trail passes had agreed to ask sledders to transport hay up to the Renshaw cabin. Once it was there, we could easily get the bales to the horses.

Dave wanted to store as many bales as possible up by the horses in case a storm cut off snowmobile access to Belle and Sundance. Dave figured that no matter the conditions, he would be able to sled to the bottom of the steep hill and then snowshoe up to the horses to feed them. I was surprised at his optimism, though not by his determination. Weather in the mountains is always the unknown, and storm conditions would confound Dave's plan at a time when the horses would be most desperate for food.

While we were unloading Stu's snowmobile and securing two bales to it, along came the two B.C. SPCA constables who'd visited the horses the day before. Kent Kokoska, a senior animal protection officer, asked me to put a sign up by the horses asking people not to feed them. I didn't have any more cardboard, so he handed me his clipboard. I made a temporary sign, which read:

> Please DO NOT FEED horses! They are being
> looked after and fed according to the vet's feed
> schedule. Too much feed will kill them! However,
> we do need help digging! Your efforts are
> appreciated. For more info, call Spin Drift.

"Thank you so much for what you guys are doing for these horses," said special provincial constable Jamie Wiltse.

*A sign to let people know the horses were being fed according
to a vet's prescribed schedule.*

The two constables didn't stay long (they were here on their vacation time) but did say that an SPCA constable from Prince George would be back on Monday with a snowmobile.

Monika then arrived in her truck. She had picked up a few more shovels donated by the local hardware store. Even though she couldn't get a ride to the horses that day, she was bent on recruitment and planned to talk to sledders in the parking lot about the horse rescue and ask them to help shovel.

Dean Schreiber and his thirteen-year-old son, Sam, had planned to come this day as well, but they hadn't been able to get their truck started either. Stu and I, it turned out, were the only diggers.

The ride up to the horses was witheringly cold that day, but at least my head stayed fairly warm since Stu had loaned me a helmet. Only my toes complained on this, the harshest day of the digging so far.

December's average temperature in this part of the valley is minus ten degrees. On December 1, the McKale weather station was reporting a high of plus one, but starting on December 13, just two days before the horses were first spotted, the temperature had turned dangerously cold, as low as minus thirty-six degrees at the weather station and four degrees colder than that at our Falling Star Ranch.

But seen another way, the cold was a blessing. I sometimes ached from the work of shovelling, but Matt, Stu and Dave never did. As shovelling went, Matt observed, this was good shovelling. Owing to the cold, the snow stayed light and powdery; anyone who has ever shovelled wet snow or slush would appreciate the difference.

When we got to the spot where the trench was to meet the groomed snowmobile trail, Stuart and I stopped and put up the two signs, one facing each way. We also left a few shovels there and put flagging tape around some of the trees to make the area more visible.

Just before noon, we stopped at the Renshaw cabin to warm up for a few minutes. I told a group of sledders inside about the horse rescue and asked them to come help shovel.

"You'll generate heat doing it," I said, hoping to entice them.

"We'll go ride first and then we'll come help for a while," said one.

I had my doubts. They were already drinking beer.

Once we reached the horses, I put my balaclavas and gloves under the hood of the sled, on top of the still-warm engine so they could dry before I started the day's shovelling. I had learned my lesson from my first day on the mountain.

As for Belle and Sundance, they already looked quite a bit better than they had two days before. When we got there, they were clearly happy to see us and gave us a soft, low whinny as a greeting. Horses housed in a barn or corral and fed according to a schedule know when breakfast comes even a minute late, and they inform everyone of their displeasure. The whinny from Belle and Sundance that morning was more of the pleading kind: "Feed us. Please, please feed us."

Jamie Wiltse had given us two more horse blankets, these ones made of thick canvas. I fed the horses and then put an additional blanket on each of them—the mare, to my pleasant surprise, actually stood still this time.

Stu, meanwhile, gathered firewood so we could melt snow to water the horses. And then we set to work on the trench.

With only two of us digging, and my having to trudge back to the campfire several times throughout the day to refill the bucket and tend the fire, we didn't make much progress. Nevertheless, we had fun. We joked with each other and teased each other, doing our best to lighten the work. "Got to keep laughing to keep from crying" best defined the day. Thursday I had felt down, numbed by the impossibility of our task. Not today. Besides, the sun was shining, the sky was a deep azure, and there was not a cloud in sight on this gorgeous clear day. And I liked Stu. He was not the sort to laugh out loud, but he seemed always to wear a smile on his face. He struck me as a man content with his lot and alive to the glories of nature. Over a Thermos of coffee or while breaking for lunch, we talked about the splendour of the alpine, the horses and their predicament, and what their owner had and had not done. Stuart was an easy man to talk to. And, like Matt, content to let others grab the spotlight.

Stu presented an idea—typical of him, it was offered as a suggestion, not issued as an order—that we quit work at the top end of the trench earlier in the day so we could spend time starting a new trench at the bottom to give people an incentive to dig from that end as well. So we worked away where we were until almost three o'clock and then returned to the horses.

Sundance still wasn't drinking, and I was a little concerned that he might suffer an impaction colic—blocked intestines from a solid mass of food. A horse needs water when fed hay. But the gelding did seem to eat quite a bit of snow. Not the same as drinking water, but better than nothing, I figured. It's true what they say: you can lead a horse to water, but you can't make him drink. After feeding the horses more hay, watering them and checking their blankets, Stu and I headed out.

I had not minded the ride in as much that day, but I was dreading the cold ride out after working up a sweat shovelling. When we got down to the groomed trail, we found a snowmobile parked to one side. The machine belonged to Jesse and Liz Trask, a young couple from McBride. Having seen our signs, they'd started work on the bottom part of the trench and had already dug from the groomed snowmobile trail to the creek. Jesse was busy flooding the creek bed to make an ice bridge.

I was pleased by the initiative, but hardly surprised. Handy and hard-working, Jesse is a mechanic by trade and a farmer. He and Liz knew exactly what had to be done, and they did it.

Under all the snow, which had acted as an insulating blanket, the water in the creek hadn't frozen yet, so it would have been impossible to cross the creek with the horses. Only a thin layer of ice lay between the snow cover and the water in the creek, which, beneath all that snow, was still flowing straight down the mountain—virtually north to south. Jesse's solution was to shovel a path about three feet wide and four feet long—running east to west. He left about a foot of snow, then made a hole in the ice, just above his path, and scooped out water, which he poured over the snow where the crossing would occur. Mother Nature would do the rest overnight; before morning, the new path would be slippery but rock solid.

Stu and I worked alongside Liz and Jesse for a while. Soon after, we heard voices. Two snowmobilers who had seen the signs we had posted had walked down the trench to investigate. They promised to talk to other sledders and come help shovel the next morning. I was skeptical. Monika had had little success mustering volunteers back in the parking lot. Owing to the bitter cold, few people were going sledding. Like me, many no doubt had had trouble starting their snowmobiles and trucks. And the beer-drinking sledders I had tried to coax into helping earlier that day never did show up. Not everyone is moved by the plight of stranded horses.

The ride out was worse than Thursday's. My toes went numb. I tried moving them around but still couldn't restore feeling. The trip seemed to take longer too, and literally it did. Stu stopped every once in a while to make sure Jesse and Liz were still behind us—a matter of courtesy and safety that, while necessary, also prolonged the journey down the mountain.

When we got to about kilometre five on the logging road, Stu stopped suddenly. In the near darkness, I couldn't see much, but I thought we were stuck. The creek, we discovered, had flooded the trail, and huge ice chunks were scattered everywhere. The water must have encountered an ice jam, and when it broke, the creek overflowed its edges. I got off the sled so Stu could manoeuvre it across the ice. By the time we arrived at the parking lot, darkness had descended, and I could hardly feel my extremities anymore. Stu's beard and moustache were white with hoar frost.

Fortunately, Stu's old Chevy—about the same vintage as my venerable Ford—started right away. While he loaded up his sled from the loading ramp, I pulled out my cellphone and was surprised to find I still had battery power left. It was a challenge to dial Monika's number with my numb, uncooperative fingers, but I got through. She was going to meet me at Stu's house and give me a ride home.

A welcome sight greeted us when we got into Stu's truck: a plastic container stuffed with sandwiches. The sandwiches were from Joette Starchuck, who had come out to the Renshaw parking lot with food and hot coffee and to keep Monika company while she tried to recruit sledders as diggers. This was one more example of someone in the community finding a way to help the rescue effort—by helping the helpers.

Stu and I didn't talk much on the way home. I was already looking ahead, laying out all the chores I had to get done.

Once at Stu's place, I positioned myself in front of the wood
stove and didn't move until I heard Monika's truck pull into the
yard. I was still frozen, still unable to feel my toes, and I barely
warmed up during the twenty-minute ride home, even though the
heater in her truck was blasting. Instead of just dropping me off at
home, Monika kindly stayed and helped me do chores.

Reg and his wife, Krys, had invited me to their place for a
Christmas party that night, but by the time I got inside after taking care of the animals, I was too tired and chilled to consider
leaving again. What I needed most was a hot shower. As well, I
had no vehicle: my truck probably wouldn't have started (I had
once more unplugged it so the horses could have water). On top of
that, countless phone messages and emails awaited replies, which
would consume most of my evening. The audience for this story
was growing steadily, and people wanted the latest information on
the rescue and on how they might help.

After my shower, I seated myself at my computer and read
through my emails. Joette, I saw, had been beating the drum. She
had contacted all the local hotels, and staff had advised her that
several sledders were going to help. Her email had come in that
morning. I felt a sense of relief that I hadn't seen it before heading

to Dave's, for the message hinted that more diggers were coming. I would have gone up the mountain full of hope, only to see that hope dashed. Joette had also alerted major TV and print media in Prince George, Vancouver and Edmonton. A national broadcaster, CTV, planned to run the story very soon—using my photos sent by Lisa Levasseur, who had also been spreading the word. As well, Joette said, an SPCA official had apparently eaten breakfast at a local hotel and talked up the rescue to sledders at the counter, who seemed keen to volunteer.

In another note, Lisa wondered if the trench we were digging posed a hazard to sledders unaware of the rescue effort. She worried about sledders getting seriously hurt, creating a major liability issue for everyone involved. Her suggestion was to place bright marker flags on wire, flagging tape and danger signs along the entire length of the trench. I questioned whether the risk was real. The horses were in a steep and heavily treed location; only the most reckless recreational sledders would go in there. Rescuers had tried describing the terrain to others back down in the valley, but you really had to see it to truly understand it.

Emails and phone calls from people offering help poured in all evening. I sought advice on handling volunteers from Rick Maitland, who had many practical suggestions: how publicizing photographs of the horses can stir involvement, how a nurse or ambulance worker at the base of the mountain could be useful, how the sledding community was key to the rescue. "PLEASE USE THE MEDIA!" Rick wrote, using capital letters to drive home the point. "Contact all of them. Put a plea out for help. Let's make this truly a Christmas gift to remember—a gift of life! The media is what is going to bring the volunteer helpers out. . . . MOST OF ALL, DON'T GIVE UP."

That evening, I checked the sledders' forum to see what people were saying about the rescue. Some correspondents worried that the trench was too narrow; one or two again argued that the money being spent on the rescue should instead go to charity. Many others were brimming with ideas: putting homemade plywood snowshoes on the horses, packing down a trail with sleds, hauling the horses out on a skimmer, using the groomer to break a trail, pulling a trailer behind the groomer, and clearing the trail with snow blowers. One correspondent wondered if we could put water on the snow to make a narrow path of ice before laying down a series of trailer mats for the horses to walk on, with the last mat being brought to the front as the horse walked over the one behind. Another suggested tying the horses to a platform of old mattresses overtop heavy plywood. Rick Maitland proposed getting a bobcat, cat or backhoe up to the logging road and digging from that end. He was not the only one suggesting the use of heavy equipment, but unfortunately, as I knew from being up there, the steep terrain and deep snow—snow that due to the extreme cold would not pack down—made that option impossible.

This kind of brainstorming offered a measure of the widespread concern in the community—and indeed, across the nation—for the horses. Although most of these ideas had already been voiced by the volunteers actively involved in the rescue—again, one had to be on the mountain to understand what we were up against— the moral support, the keen interest that so many people took, was heartening.

A McBride horsewoman (recovering from surgery and unable to help with digging) offered to provide stabling, feed, hay, medications, horse supplies and doctoring for the horses if needed. A horsewoman from Valemount spent several hours going from business to business putting up Lisa's flyers, and Marc put flyers up all over Jasper. A growing number of people in the Robson Valley and beyond were now working behind the scenes.

Four days before Christmas, the weather warmed up somewhat. It was still cold, but probably ten degrees warmer than the day before.

Over breakfast, I read an email from Elsie Stanley (Glen Stanley's wife), who was responding to a note that I had sent her along with a piece in the *Prince George Citizen* that referred to "the mystery" of two horses being up on Mount Renshaw for what the article suggested was a six-week period.

"My husband," she wrote, "spent a couple of days hiking in the Renshaw in mid-September and saw the horses—took pictures of them. He was concerned about them so contacted the RCMP. They put him in touch with the Alberta owner, and they had a chat. . . . Glen volunteered several times to go with him to retrieve the horses, and the owner suggested which day he would be coming out again. . . . Glen was out on the highway the day the fellow was supposed to be coming, and saw a red pickup from Alberta with a two-horse trailer so assumed that was him, but never heard from him again so had to assume the mission had been accomplished.

"I just happened to be talking with someone on Friday who knew of a mutual friend who had been up digging on the trail, so heard about the horses still being there. I told Glen and he's quite 'sickened' by the neglect. . . . Just wanted to tell you that the horses have been up there on toward four months, and nothing mysterious about it."

What was beginning to sink in was that several people had seen the horses alone on the mountain that fall. But for various reasons, the plight of the two horses was never brought to wider attention.

Hiker Glen Stanley did call the RCMP, but he was under the

impression that the situation would be taken care of. Had Glen, or anyone else, known that it hadn't been taken care of, they might well have called the brand inspector, put up flyers or mentioned the find to other horse people in the valley. I, for one, would have happily ridden up there in the fall with others to get those horses down. It would have been fun. But assumptions had been made, too much time had lapsed, and the logistics of any successful rescue had become much more complicated.

That morning, thankfully, my truck started. Elated, I headed to Monika's house to pick her up for that day's shovelling. In the truck, we talked about sundry matters: who might show up to shovel, the condition of the horses. Sometimes, we just drove along in silence as old friends will do.

While waiting for others to show up at the Renshaw parking lot, Monika and I talked to a group of sledders from Alberta. We asked them to come help shovel for a while.

"We're here to ride," said one.

"Believe me," I replied, "we have other things to do as well. But we can't let these horses starve." I continued giving them a hard time, but nothing seemed to come of it.

Afterward, Monika laughed to herself. "They're not going to come now," she said, "the way you talked to them."

Dave then showed up, followed by Leif. Stu had stayed behind to deal with frozen water lines at home but would try to come later. Liz and Jesse Trask had bowed out for the same reason. The intense cold was taking its toll. Dave had told me that Stu wasn't feeling well either, but later that day—a measure of his commitment to the mission—Stu came up and put his shoulder to the trench.

As we loaded hay bales onto the two sleds, I talked to Dave about Lisa's concern that the trench posed a hazard to sledders.

"The trench winds through the trees," he said. "Really, only locals know the area. I don't think we have to worry about it." I agreed.

I rode in with Dave, while Monika rode with Leif. Ice chunks still marred the trail. In the light of day, I could see the extent of the ice jam: some of the hundreds of pieces of ice were the size of portable televisions, others as big as desktops, and they were scattered over a twenty-foot section of the trail.

I had no helmet today, but even with my toque and two balaclavas, I was freezing. The wind chill on a sled in this kind of cold is mind-boggling. It felt as though somebody was pressing ice cubes to the top of my head.

As always, Belle and Sundance were happy to see us. They looked more chipper than they had the day before and whinnied a "where's my breakfast" greeting. Apparently in good spirits, they were a little spunkier than the last time I'd seen them. Although each of the horses had a flake of hay, sometimes the gelding would push the mare to one side.

"Move," he seemed to be saying.

"Make me," she seemed to reply, but ultimately she would comply.

Neither horse was shivering; the two blankets each wore seemed to be doing the trick. After feeding the horses their hay, I placed the new cardboard sign beside the hay bales, stored a few feet away from the horses.

Eight of us dug that day. Dave, Monika, Leif and I laboured at the top, and Dean, Barry, Steve Iben (another resident of McBride) and Stu, at the bottom. Mother Nature bestowed on us another stunning day up in the mountains. It was a lot warmer than the day before and, again, completely clear and still.

This day, though, was the toughest day for me so far. I started out already very tired, so every shovelful seemed like a huge effort. I kept hitting snags. At one spot, where the trench turned a narrow corner to avoid trees, I encountered roots and had to dig around and underneath them to reach the ground. Because we had milder temperatures, the snow was also starting to compact, which made for harder digging and lifting.

As well, we didn't dig according to the system we had used on

Thursday (with three or four volunteers spreading out as a team and digging only a few feet down before moving on) because circumstance cut into our numbers. At the bottom, Steve had to leave early and Stu came late. At the top, Leif, who had been using a chainsaw to trim branches that stood in the way of the trench, left when his back got sore. Monika and I, both only about five-foot-four, had a hard time throwing the snow beyond the six- to seven-foot-high walls of the trench. The snow kept falling back in, which was very frustrating. I can't say why we decided to forgo the stairway system that had been serving us so well. Maybe we succumbed to psychology. Having three diggers spread out made it seem as though we were making more progress. So Monika, Dave and I were the only ones left at the top by the early afternoon.

"Let's dig until about 2.30 p.m., then head to the other end of the trench and help the guys down below," Dave suggested.

"Sounds like a plan," I said.

We were just about to finish at the top end for the day when five sledders came walking down the trench, shovels in hand. They were the guys from the parking lot this morning.

"I guess your persistence impressed them," Monika said to me in a low voice while trying to suppress a laugh.

The sledders, young men from Alberta, shovelled for a while but within half an hour started to peter out, one after the other. One,

Birgit (left) and Monika have a rest by the campfire.

lying on his back in the snow smoking a cigarette beside his sled, eyed the sky. "Why are you doing all this?" he asked.

"The owner of the two horses thought it wasn't possible to get the horses out, but we aren't going to let them die of starvation," I explained.

"So you have to prove that it can be done," he said, sneeringly. We just smiled. This fellow clearly neither understood nor cared.

But we felt good about how much we'd accomplished. Monika

and I decided to snowshoe down so we could see how much digging was left to do. Dave loaned Monika his snowshoes, and I strapped on mine. We arranged to meet Dave at the other end of the trench, down by the groomed snowmobile trail.

Even though we'd made good progress over the past couple of days, the walk on snowshoes still seemed long. Several times we thought the creek was just around the corner, only to be disappointed. On the other hand, the going was easier than before: the trail had been walked on a few times, so it was hardening up, and we weren't sinking in as much or taking as many tumbles. When we got close to the flooded creek bed near the groomed snowmobile trail, we met Dave, who was already digging alongside Stu. The four volunteers at the bottom had probably shovelled close to a hundred metres that day as well. Dave estimated that we had about half a kilometre of digging left.

The ride out was uneventful and not as cold as the night before's. On our way home, Monika and I stopped at the Husky gas station in McBride. Feeling drained, I was longing for a Coke and a chocolate bar to boost my blood sugar level. As I stepped out of my truck, another pickup pulled up alongside us—Tim and Justin had just returned from a trip to Prince George.

Monika and I told them about our day's work.

"You are never going to get this done. There's no way," Tim said.

Stuart, Birgit and Dave stop to warm up.

Monika, also exhausted, lit into him. "This is just what we want to hear after spending the whole day up there digging," she retorted angrily. I sympathized with her. We'd suffered enough naysayers without our families and friends chiming in.

Once at home, I fed my hungry critters and ate a couple of Joette's leftover sandwiches, which tasted incredibly good—for a change, I was actually hungry. Then I set out to return phone calls (about a dozen of them) and answer emails (about two dozen). A producer at CTV had left a message; he ended up talking to Lisa Levasseur and to Donna-Rae Coatta, the media liaison for the Rescue 100 Horses Foundation. The piece aired that night. Seeing my pictures of the horses on television brought tears to my eyes. The horses didn't deserve this. I wanted them out of their icy prison. That's all I could think about and all that kept me going.

Earlier in the day, Frank Mackay had called Reg Marek to find out how things were going with the digging. He said he had two more days of work to do on his horse trailer, then he would be out here to pick up his horses. Reg said nothing. As far as he was concerned, the correct response to such gall was no response at all. I was as appalled as Reg at the owner's audacity. Did he really think he could just waltz in and pick up the same horses he had abandoned?

While many of us involved in the rescue of Belle and Sundance had had no clue in the early days who their owner was, and then later knew just his first name, Reg, as the local brand inspector, had known his name almost from the beginning. Frank Mackay called Reg five times all told, and the former left an indelible impression on the latter.

"Absolutely arrogant to the extreme" was how Reg described him.

"Some people who go up in the mountains have no clue," Reg later told me. "I give him lotsa marks for getting as far as he did—he did have some experience; he just didn't know when to quit. In Alberta, on the eastern slopes, you can get away with things. Here he was out of his league. He had no clue where a horse could go and not go. He thought the horses would come down, and that was a reasonable expectation. Often, you can't keep horses up there. It's why we sometimes hobble horses on pack trips. But in this case, there was bog. And they would not go through that misery again."

Reg had called Frank Mackay on the second day of digging to verify that the horses on the mountain were his. "He was pretty rude," said Reg. "He was prepared to leave them there to die. 'It's none of your business,' he told me, and when I challenged him, he said he couldn't shoot a cat, never mind a horse—though later he said he was a hunter."

The last thing any of us wanted to do was release those horses to Frank Mackay. Fortunately, the SPCA constable was supposed to meet us at the parking lot next day. I planned to have a chat with him about this new development. The constable never showed, but neither did the owner, so my initial feeling of panic subsided. When I mentioned to Dave that morning that the owner intended to claim the horses, he calmly advised, "Let's just deal with it as it comes."

For now, we would focus on the hard task at hand.

Chapter 9
THE TUNNEL TO FREEDOM

On Monday, December 22, I rose to another cold-snap dawn. The outside thermometer read minus thirty-one, and the radio announcer predicted a daytime high of minus fifteen.

From our living room's huge sealed window (with a major crack in one corner from the cold of a previous winter), I looked out on my universe. Panning from left to right, I could see my stallion Fire's paddock (to prevent war with the geldings or breeding with the mares, I kept studs apart from the other horses), then the chicken coop and garden shed, the little red barn, the tack shed beside it, the fifty-foot round pen for untrained horses and green riders, the vegetable garden, the guest cabin still in the works and the wide path that led down to a creek then up to the pastures and to the big outdoor riding ring—its entryway crowned by elk antlers. The soil in our pastures is clay, so it holds the moisture well, producing rich grass when the weather is kind.

Inside, as outside, horses rule at Falling Star Ranch. The soap dish, the soap dispenser and the towels in the bathroom all bear horse motifs, and horseshoes—along with hundreds of other items—adorn the shelves and walls. Monika insists I am a pack rat, and I have to admit she's right. But I am a *Swiss* pack rat, which means the hundreds of items—bottles; tobacco tins; portraits; photos, sculptures and drawings of horses, cats and dogs; the antlers on the mantel—are all arrayed just so.

Ours is a rectangular-shaped property, with the Rocky Mountains across the valley in the northeast and the Cariboos in the southwest, behind the ranch. The eyes of visitors to the property are forever drawn to the mountains. Vast wine-coloured strips run through the forests on those mountains, and to visitors they look pretty—until it's pointed out that this colour marks conifers devastated by mountain pine beetles. But even this flaw does little to taint the glory of those peaks.

Sometimes I wish we had more land, more money, a newer and better house, but other times, walking out to the horses at dawn or dusk, I pinch myself. I stare up at the sun rising over the Rockies or dipping below the Cariboos and think myself the luckiest person on the planet. There is nowhere else I would want to live than here. Some need to live near water—rivers, lakes, oceans. I need mountains.

Dozens of young horse lovers from Europe, Australia and Canada have spent whole summers at Falling Star. In exchange for work—feeding the horses, cleaning the tack, cleaning the corrals, weeding the garden, exercising the horses—the volunteer gets free board, riding lessons and all the expertise I can pass on to them, plus a chance to experience life on a Canadian horse farm. The farm exchange workers would probably agree that I possess an iron hand in a velvet glove.

My horse know-how comes from working as a guide at a dude ranch and as an assistant trainer at a warm-blood training facility. Having studied extensively under Chris Irwin, one of Canada's most celebrated horse trainers and clinicians and author of two books (*Horses Don't Lie* and *Dancing with Your Dark Horse*), I am a gold-certified trainer in groundwork and silver-certified in riding. I'm currently working on my Chris Irwin gold certification in riding as well as my Equine Canada Level 1 Western and English teaching certificates. Chris subscribes to the theory of training the trainer to think like a horse and to speak the horse's language, which is, first and foremost, body language.

~

That day, December 22, I rode up to Mount Renshaw with Dave. As usual, I looked forward to seeing the horses, but the excitement of the first day was gone. I didn't like the ride in on the snowmobile and felt anxious to get to the horses, feed them and start digging. I just wanted to get the job done.

As always, the horses greeted us with a whinny. Clearly getting pickier with their feed, they had some hay left over from the previous night's meal. With every passing day and every feeding, the gelding and mare grew more lively, more themselves. Ever so slowly and ever so slightly, they were gaining weight and shedding worry. After giving the horses their morning ration of hay, we launched into the digging routine. Matt, along with others, had grown increasingly frustrated with all the promised assistance that wasn't materializing.

"All this hype but no help," he complained.

One day—the day the vet arrived to examine the horses—Matt had walked into the Renshaw warming cabin and heard some

Tom Parviainen and Dave Jeck take a break from their digging.

Alberta sledders talking about "some people who were trying to rescue two horses up here."

"Yeah," he'd told them, "I'm part of that bunch."

Without Matt asking, the sledders offered assurances that they would lend a hand the next day, but Matt put no stock in their promises, and, sure enough, he never saw the sledders again.

"All this yak in town, all this media coverage. But why isn't it translating into diggers?" Matt asked. Fatigue and frustration had begun to wear on him, too.

But on that Monday, with Christmas three days away, all that yak yielded results. The number of volunteers mushroomed—fifteen in total. Digging at the top were Dave, Stu, Matt, Tom Parviainen (a friend of Sara's who'd learned about the rescue through Facebook) and me.

Digging down at the bottom were Linden and Logan Salayka Ladouceur (two teenage brothers), Brian McKirdy and his son Ross, Ross's friend Reiner Thoni, Barry Walline, Dean and Sam Schreiber, and Tim and Justin Brown. Just twelve, Justin was the youngest member of the shovelling brigade. Dean's son Sam was only a year older.

The work seemed easier with this many people, as if we drew energy from each other, and the mood on the mountain was ecstatic. A sense of camaraderie touched every volunteer, and jokes

Justin Brown, the youngest member of the shovelling brigade,
digs in to help free the horses.

and teasing ruled the day. Everyone was feeling good, generating lots of chatter—about the weather, about work, about the horses. The day had the feel of a joyous work bee.

Four sledders from Alberta happened upon the bottom crew and dug with them for a long time. In the snow they wrote the name of their town—Bonnyville.

Later in the afternoon, Dave used his GPS (global positioning system) to measure the distance we had shovelled that day. He figured we had dug another two hundred and fifty metres, meaning that just two hundred and fifty remained. The volunteers cheered at that news.

"If this many people show up again tomorrow, we should get it done in a day or two," Dave predicted.

Toward the end of the day, Matt, Tom and I stopped our work in the trench and began creating a new pad for the horses—simply a widening of the trench, about a third of the way to the logging road. We were thinking of moving the horses there and giving them a break before heading all the way out of the trench the next day or the one after. And we would have moved them to the new pad had it started snowing hard or blowing, but the weather remained fair, so Dave suggested we didn't need to move them after all.

After feeding the horses their supper, offering them water and checking their blankets—my end-of-the-day routine—I felt a huge sense of satisfaction. We had accomplished a lot that day. For the

*A lineup of snowmobiles near the bottom of the trench
was a welcoming sight after a hard day of shovelling.*

first time, getting the horses off the mountain looked manage-
able. I walked the short trench from the horses up to the alpine
and waited for Dave and his snowmobile. The ride out took my
breath away. Dave stopped his machine at one point so we could
admire the setting sun, which had cast the rock and snow of the

mountaintops in a striking shade of pink. I now understood why so many people own and ride sleds. The views in this high country are ones to give you pause and make you feel glad to be alive.

"I hope to come back here in the summer on horseback," I told Dave. "I want to explore some of these areas."

When we got to the bottom end of the trench, a wonderful sight greeted us: a long lineup of sleds alongside the groomed snowmobile trail and many volunteers shovelling, shoulder to shoulder.

~

Once home, I met with another pleasant surprise. Marc was back from Jasper, had done the chores and was just in the process of making supper—my first real meal in days, shrimp and rice, one of my favourite dishes. All of a sudden, I felt ravenous.

At 10:20 p.m., I sent out another update with pictures and a note that read in part:

> Hi all. Had a great day today. Only have 250 metres
> to go! The horses are doing better every day. Thanks
> to all who were up on the mountain today. . . .
>
> P.S. We have received a lot of coverage.

What I didn't know, and only discovered much later, was that Dave chatted with Belle and Sundance's owner that same evening. Dave had tracked down Frank Mackay's name and telephone number and called him. He wanted to hear Mackay's side of the story, to get the measure of him.

Dave felt some sympathy for the man, who had been demonized by the media and the public. He wondered if he was just a guy who got into trouble with his horses. The two men spoke for about half an hour, calmly and rationally. Dave was neither aggressive nor accusatory while Mackay simply told his story—how he thought he could handle taking horses to the Great Divide and never imagined how it would all turn out.

Dave believed that the owner had made valid attempts to get the horses down off the mountain, and though maybe he hadn't done all that Dave himself might have, no intentional wrong had been committed. If Mackay had left his horses tied to the warming cabin and they'd starved, that, thought Dave, would have constituted a true crime. But after speaking with him, Dave decided the case wasn't black and white.

Dave knew, and Frank Mackay knew, that all over Canada horses were abandoned and starved all the time. That night, Dave Jeck, the man leading the painstaking rescue of Belle and Sundance, thought: Why is their owner the one up on the cross?

~

After I got off the phone for the final time that night, I headed from my office to the kitchen for a restorative glass of milk, which I hoped would help wind my engines down. I passed, on my right, a cork bulletin board—home to important phone numbers, photos of horses, dogs and cats, a to-do list and much else. Halfway down the board, below eye level, is a handwritten line from *The Little Prince* (or *Le Petit Prince*, in its original French) by Antoine de Saint-Exupéry in 1943.

"You become responsible, forever," the line reads, "for what you have tamed."

In the little novel, a boy is engaged in conversation with a fox, and the fox is explaining to the boy the meaning of tame and all the joys—and responsibilities—inherent in the word. Both Marc and I believe passionately that Saint-Exupéry uttered a profound truth when he wrote that there is a contract between humans and the animals entrusted to us. This is a sacred bond, and we break it at our peril.

~

Marc had been really keen on going up the mountain and helping dig, so I was glad that he would finally get the chance to do so on Tuesday, December 23, just two days before Christmas. He had been a huge moral support for me. From the moment I had heard about those horses on the mountain, I had gone into overdrive. Too exhausted to make meals or even eat, I lost weight. Helping the horses was both physically and mentally draining—the hardest thing I have ever done in my life—and I felt so fortunate to have a partner who valued the effort every bit as much as I did.

Many of the rescuers paid a price for their participation: sore backs, frostbite, lost wages, mental anguish. On or off the mountain, volunteers felt the same—the horses never left our thoughts. The digging was actually a relief because the labour offered an antidote to all that worry. Of course, no one suffered more or longer than Belle and Sundance, and what they had endured put everything else into perspective.

Marc saw himself as part of "a fresh second wave" of diggers. He'd taken no time off work to help, for he had been convinced that snow and wind would play havoc with the rescue attempt—which he thought would unfold over several weeks at least. The notion that the digging might soon be over seemed miraculous to him. "I was convinced I'd be shovelling over the Christmas holidays," he told me as we drove to the parking lot. "This is good."

When Marc and I arrived at the Renshaw parking lot, we found Monika there with boxes full of sandwiches and trail mix, all donated by the McBride Trading Co. Moving about quickly in that minus-thirty cold, we handed out the goodies to volunteers and stuffed as much food as possible into our backpacks and coat pockets, certain we'd need those rations later.

Many locals had returned home from jobs in Alberta or up north. Former residents were likewise coming back to celebrate Christmas with family and friends. That meant we had a lot of bodies, and I was thrilled to see them. Twenty-four volunteers made the long snowmobile ride to the bottom of the trench that day to help dig from the groomed snowmobile trail up toward the horses.

It was the worst ride in yet for me. The helmet Stu had loaned me—the same one I'd used twice before—kept sliding up on my head, so most of the time I couldn't see the trail ahead. The cause, most likely, was the bumpy ride: the trail hadn't been groomed for several days, so the whole way up the mountain, I had to hold on to Stu more than usual—especially since there were no hay bales behind me this time to wedge me in. Tired from all the shovelling and hanging on, I turned and twisted my arms, trying to use different muscle groups to grip. No use. I couldn't wait for the ride to be over.

Marc's ride in with Lester Blouin was just as miserable. Putting his hands forward to hang on to Lester exposed his wrists to the cold wind, but if he didn't hang on, he risked falling off the sled. His solution was to let his arms dangle at his sides and always to watch ahead for dips and rises. "It was like riding a horse," he told me later when he could laugh about it. "I was posting and trotting—on a snowmobile."

Stu and I stopped briefly where the trench emerged onto the groomed snowmobile trail, but nobody else had arrived yet. We then continued up to the horses' pen. After we fed Belle and Sundance, a group of us started digging from the top down.

Digging from the bottom were Monika, Tim and Justin; Marc; Dave and his brother Gord; Lester; Wes Phillips; Dean, Sam and Alison Schreiber; Joey Rich and his dad, Joe; Carla Trask; Carolina and Jason Beniuk; Byron Murin; Jeff Zyda; and Matt Villmure. The last five mentioned live in Alberta, but all have a connection to McBride. Two groups of Alberta sledders also stopped to help with the digging effort. With this many people, the stair method worked to perfection.

Later on, Rod Whelpton—he owns Adrenaline Tours, a company that rents out snowmobiles and offers snowmobile tours—and Barry came walking down the trench from the direction of the horses' pen. Rod and Barry had agreed to bring a two-man TV crew up the mountain, but a few kilometres after they had left the

Tim and Monika Brown turned the rescue effort into a family affair.

parking lot, the engine on Barry's sled blew. When another sledder happened along and was told the circumstances, he agreed to join Rod in ferrying the TV crew members to the bottom of the trench, from where Matt Elliott took them the rest of the way. Barry, meanwhile, started walking back toward the parking lot by himself. He'd walked about four kilometres when another local sledder on his way up the mountain chanced by. He readily offered Barry a ride back to the parking lot. Two good Samaritans in a row.

At the parking lot, Barry unloaded one of the spare machines they had brought along for just such an emergency and rode back up the mountain. Told of Barry's trek, the Global TV crew seemed astonished. Perhaps they had never walked four kilometres in their lives.

Meanwhile, the reporter and cameraman, one of them mumbling something about the mountain air being thin, seemed anxious to leave. Maybe they feared we would try to shame them into helping.

"How do you dig with that?" Dean Schreiber had joked, pointing at the reporter's microphone, and everybody had laughed.

One volunteer worried aloud about all the media attention. What if something happened to the horses while they were being led out? How would that make us look?

"How can we look bad?" answered Marc. "We'd only look bad if we'd quit on them. You don't look bad for trying."

I agreed with Marc's sentiment, though I did still worry that the horses might balk at entering the trench. They had readily walked down a short steep trench to their new pad a week beforehand, but this new trench was far longer, with no end in sight.

~

Belle and Sundance had worked a little magic, even on people with no interest in horses—such as Barry. The avid snowmobiler and volunteer with the local search and rescue unit dug on the mountain for two days, though he later conceded with irreverent humour, "I'm not a horse person. Horses hate me. The tamest one will try to bite me. I could not believe we were doing this nonsense. I was very negative about all this in the beginning. I thought the digging was stupid, but one look at the horses . . ."

Matt had said the same thing. To see Belle and Sundance in the flesh was to sign on to the rescue team.

All over the Robson Valley, horse-mad wives were putting pressure on husbands to help. The men were often reluctant at first, then keen. Sara had convinced Matt to help by giving him what she called "the look." She said Matt wouldn't know one end of a horse from the other—though I think she put it less delicately than that. Judy Fraser had deployed a different tactic on her partner, Barry Walline. She used pure, simple logic: if the horses were suffering, he had to help. As Barry put it, "We were goaded into it."

Barry calls himself "a wuss," even though he'll go out in the small hours in a blizzard in minus-thirty temperatures—but only because he has to, he insists. As a recreational snowmobiler, he ducks cold weather. But when a sledder is reported missing, Barry will—along with his rescue unit cohorts—go to the highest point of the mountain and look or smell for a warming fire or try to catch the flash of a camera. He will yell to be heard or listen for yelling. Invariably, the lost are found.

~

On the morning of December 23, Matt hiked from the shovelled end of the bottom trench up to the shovelled end of the top one to gauge how much digging was left to do. Climbing a rugged mountain in heavy boots and sledder suit was tiring enough, but all those days of digging had taken a toll on him. Once he reached us, he let himself fall back into the snow. It was the kind of freefall that kids do just before making a snow angel.

"I am not going to do that again," he said, supremely exhausted, his eyes closed. He meant the walk up the hill.

"How far is it still?" I asked.

"It seems quite a way," he answered, "but then again, I was walking uphill."

We had started digging around 11 a.m., and shortly after noon I could hear voices. One of them was Justin's.

"Hey Birgit, we're here," he shouted.

"You'd better have a shovel and not just be walking up here to see how far we still have to go!" I yelled.

"We're shovelling," he yelled back.

Marc Lavigne and Justin Brown take a breather, just before the trench is finally finished. Digging behind them is Wes Phillips.

Yeah, right, I thought to myself, but then I saw snow flying.

"Is that where the trench is?" I called again.

"Yes, we're right here," Justin replied.

Then I could see Marc's red coveralls, and behind him Wes and Lester. A human digging chain was working its way toward us. Monika and Tim were part of that crew digging from the bottom, shoulder to shoulder with strangers—people she had never met, people who had never seen the horses. *What a great bunch*, she later told me she thought as she dug. Now and again, there comes a feeling of connectedness—to one's community, to some worthy cause. You feel as though you are a vital cog in a great turning wheel. This, thought Monika, is one such moment.

I had some orange flagging tape left, so I put up a ribbon between two trees, across the point where the upper and lower ends of the trench would meet.

"The race is on!" I challenged the bottom crew. They had far more diggers, so they had an unfair advantage. I didn't care. The end was in sight.

"Come help us dig," I urged Justin. A feeling of euphoria suffused the volunteers, with everyone laughing and joking. We all found new reserves of energy and dug faster. Snow was flying up, then down, up, then down, on both sides of the trench—as if so many unseen creatures were frantically digging tunnels. The job of finishing the trench had consumed seven days, with half the work done in the first five and the other half done in just two.

At about one-thirty in the afternoon, "the tunnel to freedom"— as some in the press had come to call it—was finally completed. Cheers went up everywhere; people took off their mitts, high-fived each other and clapped. Shouts of "We got it done!" could be heard from the whole crew. I looked at Stu, and he had "Yahoo!" written all over his face.

The tunnel to freedom.

What I felt most powerfully was relief. The shovelling, at least, was over. But my elation was checked a little by the knowledge that we had finished only phase one of the rescue. There remained two more big hurdles: getting the horses into and through that one-kilometre-long trench, and then walking the almost thirty kilometres along the logging road. So the champagne wouldn't be uncorked just yet.

Marc likened it to a hockey game. "We had come back and tied up the score, which was great. But there was still overtime."

~

Dave and Stu stoked the campfire, and we all took a short break. It was two in the afternoon. We still had plenty of time to lead the horses out.

Soon after our shared celebration and subsequent rest, the majority of the volunteers walked single-file down the finished trench to the snowmobile trail while a few of us—Dave, Stu, Gord, Matt, Leif, Lester, Marc, Monika, Tim, Justin, Carla, Carolina and I—headed back up the trench to Belle and Sundance.

Seeing the horses for the first time, Marc thought they looked forlorn and skinny, their blankets just hanging on them. The first image that came to mind was footage from the Second World War.

Lester Blouin with Sundance, and Dave Jeck with Belle,
shortly before the walk down the trench.

He remembered a camera panning across a gathering of humans and their animals, and how each bore the gaunt look of creatures who had known what it is to starve.

"You should have seen the horses a week ago," I told Marc. The blankets still looked far too big for them, but by the tiniest of increments and with each passing day, the horses were beginning to flesh out. For Belle and Sundance, deprived so long of sustenance, it was all about the food. These men and their machines had for many days now been bringing them grub, and the horses knew, just knew, they were safe. Not yet off the mountain, not yet out of the cold, but—for the moment, anyway—safe.

Dave instructed everyone left save Lester and me, who would lead the horses out, to walk ahead down the trench to the logging road. Dave was worried that if the horses encountered some mishap in the trench, those behind them would be stuck.

Belle and Sundance had their heads up and their ears pricked forward. They were two horses ready to roll. We put halters on them and removed their blankets for the trip down the narrow trench (lest the blankets get hung up on a protruding root or branch), we loaded gear onto snowmobiles, pulled strings off the remaining hay bales to be left in the high country (the polymer might have ensnared wild animals), and soon after, the two horses began their trip down the narrow passageway.

I felt the same elation as others, but mine was tempered. I still had concerns about this next critical leg of the journey. Would the horses, generally claustrophobic creatures, follow us down a slippery, one-kilometre-long trench barely wider than their bodies and surrounded by a six-foot wall of snow—especially when turning around was not an option? I worried that some spots in the trench were too narrow and that the horses might get stuck or refuse to advance. There was one section, in particular—the section where I'd had a difficult time digging because of roots buried under the snow—where we'd had to try to find the best way around a great many trees. I had hoped to widen the trench the following day, but the walls and bottom had turned to ice. I would have needed a pick.

Lester led the way down the trench, with the older gelding in tow. Dave followed with a shovel in case one of the horses got stuck in deep snow or entangled in exposed root. I followed with the young mare. Behind Belle was Gord, who picked up shovels that had been tucked into the trench walls. Marc and Monika snowshoed beside the trench, high above us. Marc was taking pictures, but pretty soon he could no longer keep up with the horses. They were just motoring down the trench. I had to walk really fast,

Lester Blouin leads Sundance through the trench.

*Dave Jeck is followed by Birgit Stutz (hidden), who leads
Belle down the mountain. Behind Belle is Gordon Jeck.*

sometimes almost run, to stay ahead of Belle. Sundance seemed a little stiff, likely from not having had any exercise in such a long time, and moved more slowly. That he was ahead of us worked to our advantage, for he slowed the mare's pace.

Some members of the sledders' forum had expressed fears that the handlers could be run over if the horses panicked in the trench. I suppose that could have happened, but Lester and I were confident, experienced handlers. With horses, calm often begets calm, and Belle and Sundance never panicked. They seemed to know we were helping them, and they'd clearly had their fill of the mountaintop.

Luckily, too, we didn't have to deal with many obstacles on our journey down the trench. Everything went smoothly, save for one time when the gelding's right hind foot slipped in the snow and under a root. Sundance practically sat down on his hind end. At this spot, the trench was not dug all the way to the ground. The snowy path was still quite soft—and probably only about three feet deep. Amid all the excitement and the great rush of volunteers, the quality of digging had suffered somewhat: getting it done mattered more than getting right to the bottom every step of the way. Because Lester reacted calmly and quickly to Sundance's plight, the gelding didn't panic. With Dave's help, Lester managed to back the gelding up and free his hind foot. The sure-footed mare had no such trouble. The horses slid a bit going down some of the steeper sections of the trench, but both remained sensible about it all. Even the creek crossing was uneventful.

At 2:45 p.m., the horses and a handful of volunteers emerged from the claustrophobic trench onto the wide, groomed snowmobile trail. Cheers and applause from all the other volunteers, who anxiously awaited our arrival—likely two dozen all told—greeted us. I remember seeing a sea of smiling faces and all these backpacks and snowmobiles and shovels on the side of the logging road. Belle and Sundance pricked their ears in response to the shouting.

But the exhilaration was short-lived. Horses and rescuers had the same question: now what? This wasn't over yet, not by a long shot. Would the two emaciated horses have the strength to walk the next and final leg—almost thirty kilometres of groomed trail—in one go? Would we be forced to stop at some point and create another temporary pen for the horses where they'd spend one more night?

We allowed the horses time to rest and again blanketed the mare, who had begun shivering. The gelding seemed fine, but we put his winter blanket on one of the sleds; it would be available when needed. Dave also tied a bale of hay onto a sled for the trip down the groomed snowmobile trail. All the remaining gear—shovels, signs, the volunteers' personal items—was packed up and loaded onto the many sleds.

Lester and Sundance emerge from the trench onto the logging road.

Then the majority of volunteers started the long, cold snow-mobile ride down the mountain to the parking lot, ahead of the two horses and their handlers. It was shortly after 3 p.m. when Gord, leading Sundance, I, leading Belle, and Marc all started the trek down the logging road. Marc soon opted to catch a ride with Tim and Justin; he could hardly walk in his "big monkey suit" (as he calls his thick winter coveralls). Poor Justin was squeezed in between Tim and Marc on Tim's rented snow machine.

Monika had thought she might be part of the group leading the horses down the logging road, but the cold had begun to bite, along with the fatigue, and her warm house beckoned.

"But promise you'll call me when you get home," she said before leaving. "I don't care what time it is." I promised I would.

Dave, meanwhile, worked on logistics. He instructed Marc to call Ray when he got down to the valley to let him know that we were on our way down with the horses. Ray would need to hook up his livestock trailer and ready the stalls in his barn in case we managed to walk all the way out.

Shovelling in the sun all day had caused Marc to sweat up on the mountain, which, because of temperature inversions, could some-times be warmer than the valley. Now, with dusk approaching, he was dropping down into the cold valley, with the speed of the sled adding yet more bite to the wind chill. Tim was driving the sled, which had handlebars for the passenger—in this case, Marc. "This is great," Marc told Tim as they sped down the mountain. "These handlebars are heated."

"Uh, I don't think so," Tim replied.

Marc thought of that short story by Jack London, "To Build a Fire," in which a man—foolishly hiking across the tundra during his first winter in the far north—fights a losing battle with minus-seventy-five-degree cold. Those who have read that story, set in the early 1900s, often remember two salient details—the man's folly in building his fire too close to a snow-laden spruce, and the great warmth that is said to come over humans just before they freeze to death:

> He must sit and rest, he decided, and next time
> he would merely walk and keep on going. As he
> sat and regained his breath, he noted that he was
> feeling quite warm and comfortable. He was not
> shivering, and it even seemed that a warm glow
> had come to his chest and trunk.

Marc remembers playing hockey on outdoor rinks near his family's home in Parry Sound, Ontario. The pain and tingling were only felt when you came inside and the warm air hit the frozen skin.

When he got to the parking lot, Marc, instead of calling Ray, drove straight to Ray's farm. Lu came to the door. Marc told her the horses were on their way.

"Great!" she answered.

When Marc explained how chilled he was, Lu, a soft-spoken, kind and generous farm wife, directed him to the basement, where a big oil furnace sits next to a wood stove. After a few minutes, she went down to check on him. Her perennial smile got a little wider when she saw Marc with his hands out and pressed close to the oil furnace.

"That's the one that's hot," she said warmly, pointing at the wood stove.

As she drove home in the dark, Monika found herself going over what the rescue had meant to her. She remembered the frantic moments in the early days, searching on the Internet for expertise on the feeding of starving horses, and how impossible the task of digging had seemed at first. Monika relived her three days of shovelling, recalling the frustration of her first day and the fun of the second, how she and her fellow diggers had come to laugh at how hard the work was and tossed snow at each other.

Dave and Birgit (with Belle) are all smiles after the successful journey down the trench.

After that day, her attitude had changed completely. The impossible looked possible after all. Digging with strangers, friends, acquaintances, she felt that they all shared a common purpose.

For many in the Robson Valley, getting those horses off the mountain would be the best Christmas present ever.

Chapter 10
HOLD YOUR HORSES

The horses were out of the woods, but not yet off the mountain. The thirty-kilometre logging road still lay ahead.

Matt, Dave, Lester and Stu—all on snowmobiles—followed Gord, me, Belle and Sundance. The four sledders stayed well behind us so they could warn snowmobilers approaching from behind them of the horses ahead. Luckily, only a few remained on the mountain, and none came by after dark.

We talked about creating a makeshift pen somewhere along the logging road and leaving the horses overnight, then coming back the next day to finish the journey. However, we worried that predators would make an easy meal of them. Wolves, cougars and coyotes avoid the alpine, preferring the lower ranges—a fact that had so far protected Belle and Sundance. This far down the mountain—and on a groomed trail at that—the threat of carnivores became much more real.

On the other hand, the horses faced a marathon walk. They had lost a lot of muscle mass during their ordeal on the mountain, both from standing still all that time and from the wasting. So much muscle had been metabolized to keep them alive. Did they possess the strength and energy required to walk the trail's full length in one go? The lost muscle left them vulnerable to bone fractures—a catastrophic thought. When we started our trek down the mountain, I tried not to think about the long march ahead of us. I just took one step, then another, and another.

The gelding was a trooper. Early on the march, he began to shiver, so we put a blanket on him. After that, he walked steadily forward. He and I were both beat, both on autopilot.

The young mare, on the other hand, was a cocky little thing. Despite her ordeal, she still had sass and attitude. Instead of walking beside me as the gelding was doing with his handler, she would drift behind me, pin her ears back in annoyance and butt my backpack with her head. Frustrated and just as annoyed as she was, I wondered what she hoped to accomplish. Maybe she was trying to

The beginning of their journey down the logging road,
with Birgit leading Belle and Gordon leading Sundance.

get at something in my backpack. I took it off and put it on one of the sleds. Her behaviour improved somewhat.

At first walking quite fast, sometimes even ahead of the gelding, Belle soon slowed down and, after a while, wanted to quit altogether. She had used up precious energy fooling around and being bold, as young horses tend to do. Several times along the way, the person leading the gelding had to get behind the mare and urge her on. Trying to pull a reluctant horse is foolish and pointless. As skinny as she was, Belle still amounted to seven hundred pounds of stubbornness. It was far easier to use the gelding's energy to press her from behind, like a tailgating motorist on the freeway urging on the slowpoke ahead. I wondered, too, if the gelding recognized the logging road—he would have come this way in the fall—and knew he was headed down the mountain.

About an hour after we started our journey, darkness began to descend. The sky was clear and full of stars, with no moon visible. Only four days to new moon. By five o'clock it was pitch dark and the temperature had dropped considerably. Only the headlamps of the snowmobiles illuminated the road. Dave suggested driving one of the sleds closely behind the horses at all times so the horse handlers had some light. At first, the horses fretted, but they soon got used to the noise, lights and proximity of the machines.

We took turns leading the horses and riding the four snowmobiles. I much preferred walking, the warmer choice. As well, I had never driven a snowmobile before, so I was reluctant. Matt, however, was encouraging.

"It's easy," he said. "I'll show you."

After some brief instruction, he left me alone with his machine while he took the mare from me. Once I got going, I was fine, but I never lost my apprehension. I worried that I'd get the sled stuck in the snow at the side of the logging road. But the cold was what bothered me most. I had loaned my big mitts to Matt while I was leading the mare—for that, my hands were kept warm enough by the two pairs of gloves I wore. When I'd handed Matt the mare's lead rope, I'd forgotten to ask him for my mitts back. Within minutes of driving the snowmobile, my hands turned ice cold. I could hardly steer and had to stop and try to warm them up by slapping them against my sides to get the blood flowing. Matt returned my mitts, but even with them, my hands weren't warming up much.

"Here, try one of these," said Stu, handing me one of those little hot packs that heat up when shaken. The heat felt wonderful, but it still took a long time for my hands to feel warm.

We stopped several times along the way to rest the horses and feed them hay. They also ate some snow. However, we had brought little food for ourselves. In my backpack, I had a half-frozen sandwich, which I ate, and a bag of chocolate-covered goodies, which I shared with the guys. The water I'd packed, though, was frozen solid.

About four hours into the journey, Stu and Matt rode ahead of us to the parking lot. Stu went to get some hot chocolate for us all, and Matt was going to call Ray Long and give him our estimated time of arrival so Ray could meet us at the parking lot with the stock trailer.

By 8:30 p.m., I was famished. Stu returned with a Thermos of hot chocolate generously spiked with Amaretto. It was so good, but I was hungry, too, and I fervently wished I had grabbed one more sandwich that morning.

We were still drinking our hot libations and the horses were munching on hay when we glimpsed the lights of a snowmobile from around the corner. It was Matt.

"I am only going to tell you guys this once, so everybody listen up," he said. His words sounded ominous, but he had certainly grabbed our attention. We moved closer to ensure we heard what he had to say. He told us that while we'd been walking, a power outage had thrown the entire Robson Valley into darkness.

"A truck tore down the power line by the Husky," Matt explained, referring to a gas station on Highway 16.

I was relieved. No big deal. Power outages are fairly common in the valley, and this one didn't affect us at all; we stood in the pitch dark anyway. But everybody following the story of the horse rescue would have been disappointed to miss the airing of the Global TV footage of the digging earlier that day. As for us on the mountain, we had our priorities: get the horses safely down, get ourselves into bed and let sweet sleep come.

About half an hour later—Dave and I were leading the horses then—we saw lights coming toward us again. This time they belonged to a pickup truck.

Wes Phillips, who lives near the Blackwater Road, had brought us hot coffee and soup.

"We're good for now, thanks," I said. I was very hungry, but I needed solids—not more liquid. "But we'd all love a warm drink once we get to the parking lot!" Wes agreed to meet us there in about an hour or so and started backing his truck down the single-lane logging road. About thirty minutes later, I again saw lights, but their angle didn't seem right.

Wes had been crossing a water bar when the ice underneath gave way and the truck sank in. Water bars are diagonal channels cut across roads on slopes like this to divert water and prevent erosion. My first reaction was relief that we had decided against trying to pull a horse trailer up the logging road. We would never have made it.

The truck blocked most of the road. Dave and I barely managed to get around it with the two horses. Gord, Stu, Matt and Lester stayed behind and tried to help Wes extricate the truck, unfortunately to no avail. Wes ultimately left it and joined our crew. He decided he would take a shift walking, so he took the mare's lead rope from me while I rode with Matt. By then I'd realized just how tired, cold and hungry I really was. We were still five kilometres from the parking lot.

The horses were doing fine, or so it seemed. The lights of the sleds behind were showing the way when I suddenly noticed that Sundance was limping ever so slightly. We stopped the march and had a look. The cut, on one hind leg, was very minor. "A long way from the heart," as cowboys say. Twice on the logging road he had broken through; he might've cut himself on a chunk of ice. Or he may have clipped himself while in the trench. In any case, the cut was of no consequence, and Sundance soldiered on.

Belle, as before, needed a push now and then. I would sometimes have to flick a rope at her hind end to keep her going. She would stall, I would send out the rope, and she would pick up her pace again. I was miffed, but so was she. Did she pin her ears to show how put out she was? Perhaps. It was too dark to tell. More likely, she swished her tail, a lesser show of objection. And so it went, kilometre after kilometre, down, ever down, the dark mountain.

Along the rest of the way, Matt and I talked to pass the time and help us forget about the cold. He told me about a trip he had taken to Europe a few years before and the different places he had visited. I leaned back on the snowmobile and stared up to the clear sky with its innumerable stars, cold distant suns that offered such scant light that I couldn't see my hand in front of my face.

About an hour later, when we were close to the end of the logging road, I asked Matt to stop, and I got off the snowmobile to

Lester visits with Belle.

walk the last few metres with Wes, Dave and the horses. I needed to warm up. The others raced ahead on their sleds.

At 10 p.m., the tired but happy group of volunteers reached the end of their seven-hour-long journey. Ray, his daughter Janice and her son Alex were waiting for us on Mountainview Road with the stock trailer. The horses loaded without incident, and at last, Belle and Sundance were on their way to a place that would resemble home: a stall in a barn, bedding to lie on, food and water. My shoulders relaxed, and I breathed a sigh of relief. It was over. There were no tears at that moment, no sense of celebration—only a barely felt happiness that we had rescued the horses without mishap.

The rescue had unfolded in three stages—digging the trench, walking the horses through that trench and walking them down the logging road. We were all happy at the end of each stage, and that happiness would have stretched into joy—had we not felt so exhausted and so wary of what lay around the next corner.

Dozens and dozens of photographs taken during those eight days chronicle the rescue of Belle and Sundance. One image captures the apple cheeks of young Justin Brown as he helped dig what looked like the world's longest, deepest and thinnest driveway. Another records the moment on December 18 when Belle and Sundance got their winter blankets (as bright and blue as the sky) and then the moment a few days later when the horses got second blankets overtop (these in muted shades of green). One photo shows a bedraggled Belle nuzzling the arm of an amused Lester Blouin. Another documents Sundance and Gord, Belle and me walking down the groomed logging road, the snow at our level looking slate blue in the fading light, the alpine and the mountain behind and above us still sunlit and so, so majestic. What strikes me most is how, as the trench neared completion and the rescue was looking more and more like a success, the weary diggers managed to smile for the camera. The horses, especially Belle with all her missing fur, look dreadful in some shots, yet it was clear that the two pack horses had literally dodged a bullet.

Rescued horses, like rescued dogs, somehow know that they have been spared a horrible fate. Belle in her way, and Sundance in his, would be grateful for the rest of their lives.

~

"When you go up in the mountains on pack trips," Dave had told me as we walked that final leg, "every day, you hope your day goes well and you don't run into trouble." He had harboured concerns that if we had dug the trench too deep, and the ground below wasn't frozen, we would have encountered mud. He had also worried about the creek crossing. But his worries were over: everything had gone beautifully. When Dave saw how well the horses moved through the trench, he knew they could handle the long trek down the logging road. It was the stamina of the human handlers he questioned—yet they, too, had come through. But there was nothing left in our tanks. Nothing.

I didn't say a lot after we loaded the horses onto Ray's trailer. "Thanks for picking us up" was all I could muster as I sat slumped in Ray's truck, the heater blasting.

~

Sara Olofsson, meanwhile, had donned several sweaters and was sitting on her couch in the cold and the dark. Her children (Logan, ten, and Emily, eight) were bunking with friends that night. Because there was no reliable cellphone service on Mount Renshaw, Sara had no way of getting in touch with Matt. He was always home from digging by 6:30 p.m. It was already 10:30 p.m. and he still wasn't home, so she knew that either something had gone horribly wrong or everything was going just right.

Matt had actually phoned and texted her four hours earlier: "The horses are being walked out." When she finally got the message, delayed as cellphone service in the mountains often was, Sara started to cry. *They're out!* she thought. *They did it!* And Sara had what she conceded was a selfish thought: Matt wouldn't have to dig tomorrow. For her, this was a wonderful Christmas gift—the knowledge that the horses would soon be warm, snoozing in a stall or dining on hay. They could have been dead and frozen, their bodies stiff, for lack of someone doing the right thing. But they weren't, thought Sara, because a great many people did do the right thing.

~

~

Exhausted, I had thought I would be heading straight to my bed once home. But I was too wired to sleep. Several media outlets had called and left messages. There were also emails from the Canadian Press wire service, the *Edmonton Journal* and others, all wanting updates on the horses. CBC Newsworld, out of Toronto, wanted to do a five-minute, live television interview the following morning. From all across Canada, from Tulsa, Oklahoma, to Orlando, Florida, from Austria to Australia, reporters would all ask the same questions: How did you manage that feat? How are Belle and Sundance doing? Why did you take on this superhuman effort? How does it feel to have succeeded?

Once the media had gotten wind of the dramatic events on Mount Renshaw, I became a point person for the story. At Christmas, the world wanted an uplifting story, and it seemed that the "heroic" rescue of Belle and Sundance—right in our own backyard—was the one that people were warming to in December of 2008.

I never expected this attention, and I found it overwhelming. When we handed Belle and Sundance over to Ray Long, I thought my job was done. I was looking forward to a day off, going into town and finally doing some Christmas shopping with Marc. Instead, I spent the day on the phone, finally stopping at 4 p.m.

Chapter 11

SOFT LANDINGS FOR BELLE AND SUNDANCE

W hile the rescuers marked their Christmas, Belle and Sundance recuperated in the barn at Ray and Lu's farm on Jeck Road. Throughout the digging process, Ray had provided bales of hay to the rescuers (without charging a penny), so the two horses had grown well used to the fare.

"They're skin and bone," Ray told Marc when he swung by for a visit just a few days into their stay. Marc had promised himself that every time he passed Ray's place he'd stop in and say hello to the horses. Ray took Marc into the barn, and the men leaned in and eyed the two horses in the large stall they shared.

"They're tight," Ray said. "If you take one away, they both complain."

Marc thought the horses looked content. He rubbed Sundance's head, then went on his way. A few days later, Monika also went to visit them and reported watching Sundance playfully bite Belle. It lifted her heart just to see them.

~

Having grown fond of Belle and Sundance, we volunteers hoped and expected that the two horses would remain together and that new owners in the valley would take them in. If the rescue itself was a gift, that outcome would have been the bright bow on the wrapping. But according to the SPCA, there'd been only a few local inquiries about adopting the rescued horses. Meanwhile, Frank Mackay was making it known in the press and by calls to Reg, the brand inspector, that he wanted his horses back.

The SPCA, it seemed, wanted the situation resolved quickly, for just one day into the horses' stay, the SPCA declared that Belle and Sundance would be transferred to a foster home in Prince George.

But five days later, Toni Jeck and a friend—both hired by the SPCA to transport the horses—arrived at Ray's farm and, with a vet's blessing, loaded Belle and Sundance. Though temperatures had risen slightly, Ray was not pleased. What was the rush, he wanted to

Sundance (left) and Belle settle into the rescue farm in Prince George.

know. Sure, the two horses wore blankets, but they were still weak from their ordeal and now would face almost three hours in that cold trailer. Ray insisted that Toni tie a tarp over the trailer's open places to reduce wind chill and stop any snow from swirling in.

During the entire rescue, most of the volunteers hadn't a clue as to the identity of the person who owned Belle and Sundance—nor did we know the names of the horses themselves. All we knew was that the owner was an Edmonton lawyer named Frank. This information had come from Stan Walchuk, who had loaned this man two pack horses on a failed expedition to find the horses in October, and from Glenn at Spin Drift.

Reg, however, had known the owner's full name even before I headed up Mount Renshaw for the first time: the brand office had received the name from the McBride RCMP. Confidentiality rules, though, meant Reg couldn't tell any of us. Then, on Christmas Eve, CTV News aired an interview with the horses' owner, but the segment used just his voice—no picture, no name. This interview revealed to us the horses' names. It was nice, finally, to know their real names—but not critical. Renshaw and Reggae had worked just as well as "the gelding" and "the mare."

I learned the owner's name in early January of 2009 by contacting a TV reporter who was covering the story. Frank C. Mackay, it turned out, was born in New Glasgow, Nova Scotia. The son of a doctor, with a science degree from McGill University and a law degree from Dalhousie University, he had practised law with the Edmonton law firm of Cummings Andrews Mackay for some thirty-two years. The firm was founded in 1915 by a lawyer who would go on to become the Attorney General of Alberta. The focus of the firm was litigation following injury or accident, though Mackay himself—according to the firm's website—was, at sixty-three, the firm's senior solicitor, with "a wealth of experience in the area of real estate, corporate/commercial law and estate matters."

~

One Alberta journalist, perhaps one of the few reporters to do so, actually visited Frank Mackay's farm southwest of Edmonton. Daniel Z. Jacobs was researching a piece for a weekly newspaper called the *Fitzhugh*. The article he wrote for the January 8, 2009, issue was startling on several counts. Mackay's candid opinions stood out for one thing; his salty language for another.

Daniel was mystified by his encounter with the man, and certain details remained fresh in his mind months later when he and I spoke.

"Is this Frank Mackay?" Daniel had asked him on the telephone before the meeting.

"It depends on who's asking," came his reply. "What's your agenda?"

Daniel told him he had no agenda, that he was a twenty-six-year-old reporter who had ridden horses as a child. He wondered if he might come to the farm and interview Mackay there. Mackay agreed.

When Daniel arrived, the horses on the farm looked to him to be healthy and happy. The photo that accompanied Daniel's story showed Mackay looking very much the rancher—brown wool hat on his head, orange scarf at his neck, an open brown checked shirt over several layers below and light-blue jeans stuffed into high boots. He was standing under a brilliant sky in a snowy paddock with a blue-eyed grey called Frank (named after the blue-eyed singer, Frank Sinatra). The horse, one of nine that Daniel counted on the farm, nosed around Mackay's pocket, as if looking for a treat.

The reporter observed on Mackay's forehead a large gash—the aftermath, Mackay explained, of an accident while driving home from Mount Renshaw on December 5. Daniel wondered privately whether Mackay had suffered a concussion in the accident and whether the head injury might explain his subsequent behaviour.

During the interview at the farm, Daniel asked, "Why didn't you hire a trapper to find the horses and put them down?" Mackay turned the air blue with his reply. Daniel later huddled with his editor to edit out some of Mackay's more profane utterances. The story, published under the title "Equine examination: McBride horse story more complicated than it seems," nonetheless conveyed Mackay's salty language.

Up on the mountain, however, the whereabouts of the owner was a common theme. Where was he, rescuers had asked, when they were there digging for eight numbingly cold days? Couldn't he at least have come by with hot drinks? And would, as many rescuers hoped, the B.C. SPCA lay charges of abandonment and cruelty causing pain and suffering?

～

Near the end of January 2009, two things happened at more or less the same time. Charges of animal mistreatment were indeed laid against Frank Mackay, and the horses found new homes. Once the abandoned horses had been seized by the SPCA, their previous owner lost any chance of recovering them. They would stay at the Prince George Rescue Farm until responsible and caring new owners could be found. No matter how the courts decided, one thing was certain: Belle and Sundance weren't going back to Frank Mackay.

Belle landed—and what a strange and wondrous coincidence this was—in the hands of Kim Gilbeau, whose daughter, Stacie Hewitt, is a friend of Gord Jeck, who had helped dig the trench on Mount Renshaw. But Kim learned this only much later.

It made her blood boil when she found out how Belle and Sundance came to be on the mountain. But it wasn't pity that made this woman fall in love with Belle.

Kim and her husband live on a ranch near Red Rock, about twenty-eight kilometres south of Prince George. Belle, or Bella, as Kim came to call her (the Italian suits the mare better, she thought), arrived at Prince George Equine Rescue in early January of 2009, along with Sundance. One day, the rescue unit's trailer arrived at Kim's place to deliver a horse she was going to foster. Belle and Sundance happened to be on that trailer (they had gone to the vet for a checkup), and both horses were unloaded to make way for the foster horse. Kim herself ended up unloading Belle. Right away she fell for her. She thought the mare looked good but terribly skinny. What Kim loved immediately was her personality, her soft affectionate manner, and the way the mare had sidled up to her. She made inquiries about adopting her, and following some

*Birgit rides Belle on a Rocky Mountain trail during
Belle's stay at Falling Star Ranch.*

SPCA visits to her ranch, the papers were signed. Belle became a Valentine's Day present from Kim's husband, Tom.

Kim and Tom have seven horses on their ranch (including one who is thirty-six years old!). The herd—with Belle and a gelding in charge—has the run of a hundred acres of pasture and bush. Kim, who calls herself a novice rider, planned to have me train Belle at Falling Star in the spring of 2010. Once she had a few miles on her, Belle would become a cutting horse and trail horse. Kim wasn't sure about her breeding but guessed by her big feet that she is a blend of quarter horse and maybe Belgian or Percheron.

The hair on Belle's belly—where she made contact with snow during all that time on the mountain—is now tinged with white. That bleaching might remain with her all her life, a reminder of what she endured.

By spring of 2010, Belle weighed thirteen hundred pounds; the bony mare I first saw on Mount Renshaw was some six hundred pounds shy of that. Kim said that when Belle first arrived at the ranch, she was very possessive of food. Woe to any other horse who came near her at mealtime. She soon became less food-aggressive and—to Kim's delight—incredibly affectionate with humans. "When she sees me," Kim said, "she'll rest her head on my shoulders. She loves the attention." That and apples and carrots and those once forbidden alfalfa cubes have worked wonders.

As for Sundance, he, too, landed softly—on an eighty-acre ranch called Poplar Springs near Kamloops in south-central British Columbia. His new owner, Catie Ward, has been riding horses since she was a kid growing up in southwestern Ontario, where she

Sundance at his new home on a ranch near Kamloops.

rode bareback. Catie has three other horses—all rescue horses—grazing her forty acres of mixed pasture, but it wasn't long before Sundance was top horse in the herd.

"Sunny is in charge of the world," Catie told me. "He's definitely the leader. But he's such a gentle giant, a true gentleman and such a source of enjoyment for us. He's so sweet. He's a big doll—with the biggest head I've ever seen on a horse. I adore him. He's the best, and I'm blessed to have him in my life."

Unlike Kim, Catie—who volunteers with the SPCA—was well aware of Belle and Sundance's story as it unfolded. A friend, a cruelty investigator with the SPCA, showed Catie pictures of the starving horses. As soon as she saw the photograph of Sundance, she knew she had to have him. When he first came to her ranch in early March of 2009, he, like Belle, was very protective of his food. And, like Belle, he would eventually become more relaxed at mealtimes. In the spring of 2010, Sundance weighed fifteen hundred pounds; he, too, had gained six hundred pounds since coming off the mountain.

Sundance will one day be a trail horse for Catie's youngest daughter, Sarah. "He has a tendency to startle a bit," Catie said, "so we'll work with him to gain confidence and trust."

In the meantime, like Belle, Sundance has been enjoying his treats: soaked beet pulp, apples and carrots in abundance.

The reader unfamiliar with horses may wonder whether two creatures that bonded as Belle and Sundance clearly did might pine for one another when separated. It's true that horse pals will show signs of distress when one is removed from the other: they may call out to that lost friend in hopes of being heard; they may pace or eat less for a few days. But horses are wonderfully resilient creatures, and they quickly make new friends and attach to another horse— which is precisely what Belle and Sundance did soon after settling into their new digs.

AFTERWORD

On February 24, 2009, following a lengthy B.C. SPCA investigation, Frank Mackay was charged with three counts of animal mistreatment—two counts under the Criminal Code of Canada (causing unnecessary pain or suffering to an animal and willful neglect in the feeding or care of animals) and one count under the British Columbia Prevention of Cruelty to Animals Act (causing an animal to be or to continue to be in distress). If convicted of the more serious Criminal Code offences, he could face a maximum fine of $10,000, up to five years in jail and a prohibition on owning animals.

Mackay was to make his first court appearance in McBride provincial court on June 12, 2009, but that was adjourned to August 14, and then once more to October 2. Some wondered if the case would ever be heard. Finally, on December 4, 2009, almost a year after the rescue, the erstwhile owner of Belle and Sundance faced the music.

There is no actual courthouse in McBride, but about five times a year a provincial court judge comes to town and sets up shop in the village council chambers, housed in a one-storey strip mall. The room used is modest, with high-backed faux leather chairs and armrests for the judge and court officials, low wooden chairs for everyone else, a framed picture of the Queen flanked by the provincial and national flags to lend the room a little gravitas and, finally, that traditional symbol of authority—a judge's wooden gavel resting on a sound block.

Mackay's court appearance marked the first time I saw him in the flesh—a compact man of average height with light blue eyes, receding grey hair and a ruggedly handsome face.

Light snow was falling when he arrived at the chambers around 10:00 a.m., with his lawyer, Alexander Pringle. One lawyer defending another, with seventy-four years of experience between them. He looked decidedly uncomfortable and, as far as I saw, made eye contact with no one.

The docket that day was full, as were the chambers. Several men and women were there to attend to their own brushes with the law—some to contest traffic tickets, some charged with more serious matters—and many others were family and friends of those so charged. Along with one of my farm workers, plus Ray and Lu, I was there to hear item number six on the judge's list—the Queen versus Frank Mackay. So too was the editor of the *Jasper Fitzhugh*. As far as I knew, the five of us were the only ones present specifically to witness the meting out of justice to Frank Mackay.

The first order of business was to hear the charge. Mackay's lawyer and the Crown prosecutor, Geoffrey McDonald, had before this day engaged in plea bargaining. In this process, the accused agrees to plead guilty to a lesser charge in order to spare both sides the time, expense and uncertainty of a trial. What then goes to the court is called "a joint submission." The two lawyers had agreed that the two more serious Criminal Code charges, which would have branded Frank Mackay with a criminal record, would be dropped. But the accused would plead guilty to the third charge, which was read aloud in court:

> Frank Mackay, between the 11th day of September, 2008,
> and the 23rd of December, 2008, at or near McBride, in
> the province of British Columbia, being a person responsible

for an animal, to wit: horses, did cause or permit the horses
to be or continue to be in distress [that's contrary to a
section of the Prevention of Cruelty to Animals Act,
Section 24 (1)].

The judge asked Mackay how he would plead. Mackay, discom-
fited, replied, "Yes, sir, I plead guilty." McDonald then laid out the
story as he understood it. Calling the case "rather well known," the
lawyer said that "the Crown takes issue with Mr. Mackay's conduct"—telling the RCMP in mid-September he'd be around to
deal with the horses "the following weekend," then not returning
for six weeks. Then, when the accused did finally locate them early
in December, the Crown considered unacceptable his decision to
"let nature take its course." Starvation, McDonald reminded the
court, "is a rather nasty way to go."

I had bristled the first time I'd heard Frank Mackay say it—"I
let nature take its course"—when I interviewed him for the newspaper on January 7 of 2009. I bristled to hear it again in court that
day. Many in the Robson Valley—and certainly the rescuers and
diggers—strongly felt that nature hadn't put those horses on that
mountain. Frank Mackay had.

The Crown prosecutor told the court that Mackay had provided
his office with pictures of the horses on the trip. Two local horse

experts had determined by examining the photos that the horses were in good health and well trained at the beginning of the trip.

When it was time for Mackay's lawyer to address the court, Pringle stated that his client had practised law in Edmonton since 1970 and was "well known in the Edmonton legal community as being a very highly regarded, ethical and responsible lawyer." Mackay had during the past ten years been involved with two charities—the Tegler Foundation, which finances homes for seniors, and Meals on Wheels—and was known as "an extremely generous person who . . . normally would give the shirt off his back to somebody."

Ten years ago, Pringle noted, Frank Mackay purchased three horses who were supposed to go to slaughter. He bought an acreage and acquired more horses. In September of 2008, Pringle said, Mackay had agreed—"as a fairly noble gesture"—to bring food to a friend who was hiking the Great Divide. It would be his first foray into the high country by himself, and Mackay thought that such a trip would offer a good experience for his horses too. The rest of the story that Pringle outlined was familiar to me: the muskeg encounter, the pack horses' no longer following their owner, the two attempts to retrieve them and the decision not to euthanize the horses but to abandon them on the mountain.

"The irony," Pringle told the court, "is that the horses survived by that decision. I am not saying it was the right decision. He has obviously made an error in judgment here. . . . He, upon reflection, recognizes there is more that could have been done."

Pringle also described the single-vehicle accident that befell his client as he made his way back to Edmonton that December night in 2008. Mackay's vehicle went off the road, leaving him with a significant cut on his head and a concussion. "He was in disarray," the lawyer said, "for a couple of weeks thereafter."

According to Pringle, Frank Mackay's "error in judgment" had cost him dearly. He had received threats, been reported to the Alberta Law Society and been brought before the court. "For a man," said Pringle, "who has never been engaged in any untoward behaviour before, this has been a harrowing experience, and he certainly regrets this event greatly and comes before you remorseful." Mackay, said the lawyer, had "learned a lesson" from "this entire series of events."

Through his lawyer, Mackay made a statement to the court, which read, in part:

> Your Honour, eighteen months ago I knew only that
> McBride was on the Yellowhead between Edmonton
> and Prince Rupert. This is now my sixth visit to McBride
> and area. In this time, I have had the opportunity to speak
> personally or by telephone with many members of the

community, whom I have found to be understanding, sympathetic, friendly and helpful. In particular, I wish to thank a local cowboy who loaned me two pack horses in my attempt to locate the horses . . . as well as the brand inspector who kept me advised to the progress of the volunteers who rescued the horses. . . . And most importantly, I wish to thank the rescuers who volunteered their time and effort to rescue these horses, which demonstrates the total unselfishness and community spirit of the citizens in the McBride area. It must have been a great feeling of contribution and success to bring these horses to safety, and, of course, it made a great Christmas story for all. If it had not been for the accident, I would gladly have participated in the rescue.

With Pringle's remarks finished, Judge Michael Gray asked him if his client had contacted the RCMP or the authorities after the two failed attempts to retrieve his horses.

Mackay spoke up. "No."

"No, he didn't, sir," said Pringle.

"I see," the judge replied.

"He tried to do it on his own," Pringle added.

The Crown lawyer rose to point out that had the accused made those contacts at the appropriate time, this matter would most likely not have come to court.

When the judge asked Mackay if he had anything to add, he replied, "No, I am fine. Thank you, sir."

By this point, an hour had lapsed. The judge said he needed time to consider documents and photographs gathered as evidence in the case. He adjourned court until just before noon.

When court returned to session, Judge Gray looked straight at Mackay. "This was a notorious case in terms of publicity," he said, "and it was a notorious case in terms of the actions that were not taken for the protection of those animals."

He continued by addressing the "entirely inappropriate" comments attributed to Mackay in the press. "I understand from your apology today that you regret your behaviour in a number of aspects, but it seems to me after the investigation was commenced and after the incident received that large national publicity, you still conducted yourself in a way that was regrettable and certainly not professional." Such behaviour, the judge stated, was unbecoming of "an officer of the court" who was potentially under investigation and facing possible charges.

Judge Gray also addressed the wider issue of horses being abandoned as a matter of practice. "That is a difficulty we have in the more remote regions of our country. In the backcountry, outfitters often take steps where they abandon horses. It is not acceptable, but it is done. . . . Where found out, it needs to be remedied."

The judge reprimanded Mackay for not contacting the RCMP and other authorities after his two failed attempts to retrieve the horses. "You did not follow up with that, which leaves me with the impression that you had made a business decision to just leave matters as they were."

In handing down his decision, the judge said he was taking into account Mackay's record as a "lawyer of longstanding and good repute, and there is no criticism to be made there." In administering punishment, the judge also considered the psychological trauma that Mackay had already endured, his age and the trauma he'd suffered from his accident. Judge Gray wondered aloud if the concussion "may have led you to conduct yourself in that regrettable fashion."

Frank Mackay was ordered to pay a $1,000 fine, a $150 victim fine surcharge and restitution to the B.C. SPCA in the sum of $5,910.16, an amount representing the cost of vet exams during and after the rescue and the cost of transporting and temporarily boarding the horses. Mackay was also prohibited from owning any animals for two years (but only in British Columbia, the only province where the judge had authority), given a probation order for two years and ordered to undergo counselling—"to ensure that there is a proper response to mental health issues" and to educate Mackay on the proper care and custody of animals. Had Mackay lived in British Columbia, and not Alberta, the judge said he would have insisted that Mackay complete a course offered by the B.C. SPCA.

The judge further instructed Mackay to deliver a copy of his probation order to the nearest SPCA office in Edmonton and to the provincial SPCA office in Alberta to alert authorities there. He was also to purchase an advertisement in two issues of our local weekly newspaper to publish the statement that his lawyer had read in court. The notice, addressed to "Residents of McBride and area" and signed by Frank C. Mackay, would appear in the *Valley Sentinel* early in February 2010.

~

Reaction to the news was swift and varied. Some thought the penalty should have been far more severe, others thought justice had been served, and some believed the proceedings were beside the point—that Mackay had suffered enough. At least Belle and Sundance would never return to their previous owner, and many of us took consolation in that.

However, the case of the Queen versus Frank Mackay was not to end there. Mackay appealed the judge's ruling about probation and counselling, arguing that Judge Gray lacked the authority to impose either. Early in February of 2010, a provincial Supreme Court judge in Prince George agreed with him.

The backdrop to all this, and it may well have figured in Mackay's thinking (and fuelled his anger at the public outcry), was a long history of kept horses starving in British Columbia. Certain outfitters simply abandon horses in the wilderness come fall ("standard business practice" was how Shawn Eccles of the SPCA put it); individual horse owners leave their horses in winter paddocks without adequate food and water (increasingly so in hard economic times); and on some First Nations reserves, where horses are often deemed common property, horses are sometimes left to fend for themselves all winter long. Such horses survive mild winters but many succumb during long or harsh winters. Even veterinarians have been caught up in charges of neglect and abuse of their own horses.

~

On February 20, 2009, a ceremony and luncheon were held in Prince George to honour the rescue effort, with Premier Gordon

At an award ceremony in Prince George (from left): Joey Rich, Deputy Premier Shirley Bond, Dave Jeck, Ray Long, Rod Whelpton, Premier Gordon Campbell, Birgit Stutz and Marc Lavigne.

Campbell and Deputy Premier Shirley Bond both present to hand out certificates. The premier and his deputy were in town on other business, but the local chamber of commerce and Bond's office used the occasion to recognize "the shovel brigade."

Though not keen on going to the ceremony, Marc and I feared it would reflect badly on McBride and the rescue group if only a few turned up, so we went. At first, we'd thought it would be fun to go on a trip with our fellow rescuers, as some of them we knew barely or not at all. Unfortunately, only a handful of them were able and willing to come. We didn't talk much about the rescue; however, we did share horse stories and sledding stories and enjoyed a lot of laughter.

The certificate from the federal government, with the insignia of the thirteen provinces and territories as well as that of the House of Commons all ringing the document, read:

> In recognition of your heroic efforts to rescue two
> stranded horses from certain death in the Robson
> Valley. Your exceptional compassion for animals
> and determined actions won the admiration and
> gratitude of the entire nation.

The provincial certificate, topped by a sun rising over a mountaintop ("British Columbia: The Best Place on Earth," it read below the drawing), stated:

> The Province of British Columbia gratefully acknowledges
> the selfless contribution made by [name inserted] to the
> December 2008 Renshaw horse rescue. Your compassionate

actions are an example of the spirit that truly makes British Columbia the Best Place on Earth.

Several of those who had either dug on the mountain or played behind-the-scenes roles were there: Dave Jeck, Ray Long, Rod Whelpton, Joey Rich, Marc and me. We all received certificates with our names on them.

There was one funny moment and, of course, Ray was at the centre of it. One by one, we were called up to the stage to be congratulated and handed our certificates. Ray was summoned last. Shirley Bond introduced Ray, whom she had met in McBride on another occasion. She shook his hand, and Ray gave Shirley a big hug. When Ray turned to shake the premier's hand, Gordon Campbell walked toward him and spread his arms, prepared for a hug. Ray, however, gave him a shove, grabbed his hand and shook it firmly, then slapped the premier in the chest.

"Oh, you northern boys are all the same," said the premier, laughing. The room broke up. Ray later explained his action this way: "I don't like being hugged in public." Not by men anyway.

That spring, I received a letter from the B.C. SPCA's Vancouver office. It read, in part, "Each May, the B.C. SPCA holds an award ceremony. . . . We honour individuals who have made an outstanding contribution to animal welfare in B.C. in the previous year. . . .

*Accepting the British Columbia SPCA Award of Heroism on behalf of the
community of McBride (from left): Mayor Mike Frazier, Birgit Stutz,
Lana Jeck, Dave Jeck, Lester Blouin and Stuart MacMaster.*

One of the major awards is an Award of Heroism, and this year the
B.C. SPCA would like to present this award to the amazing people
of McBride who rescued Belle and Sundance."

Kent Kokoska, one of the SPCA officials working out of Kamloops
who had come to see the rescue effort, said, "We were very pleased that
such a huge undertaking had been accomplished in such a short time
due to the compassionate efforts of the locals. It struck a deep chord
with us. It is something we won't forget any time soon."

"If you own an animal," said Debbie Goodine of British Columbia's SPCA in Prince George, "and that animal is suffering, it's your

responsibility to ensure that suffering is relieved." She called the rescue effort on Mount Renshaw "a miracle."

~

The story of Belle and Sundance had spread—through the Internet, through Facebook, through emails that skipped around the world. At the height of the rescue story, the sledders' forum got fifty thousand hits. The role of technology in this story taking off could not be overstated, but when all was said and done, it was local people who literally came to the rescue.

Looking back, I marvel at all our good luck. The notoriously fickle mountain weather co-operated, offering a steady stream of cold, clear days. Had temperatures risen, the snow would have turned wet and heavy and the digging would have been that much harder on our backs and shoulders. Although the cold was a burden on both the horses and the humans up on that mountain, as each phase of the trench was completed, the deep freeze hardened the track. And though I wish we had arrived sooner, we were fortunate that the horses had survived the frigid temperatures long enough for us to discover them.

The one-kilometre-long trench allowed access for Belle and Sundance, but it might also have created a passageway for predators.

Yet no predators found them. No snow fell during the eight-day rescue operation, nor during the night, and we were spared those fierce mountaintop winds that might have filled in our trench in minutes. Some days, wind rocked the valley floor but not the mountaintop. Two days after the rescue was complete, both snow and wind returned and blithely swallowed up our trench.

The early days of the rescue were a muddle, with the right hand sometimes not knowing what the left was doing. But it all worked out; the little tensions, the politics and cliques that can divide a group and lead to argument all were quickly dealt with before they could amount to anything. The abiding sentiment was this: what's best for the horses? Horses in a herd have to sort themselves out, and looking back, I can see that everyone involved in the rescue effort did the same. In fact, I was amazed at how people managed to put their differences aside. How virtual strangers formed an alliance. In a way, it was a blessing that we needed eight days to dig that trench and walk the horses out. Belle and Sundance were given time to begin gaining back the weight they had lost, to recover some of their strength, to get warm again thanks to blankets and hay. And the people working toward their rescue had the opportunity to bond.

One striking thing about this story is that it brought together three parties—those who love animals, those who love machines and those who love both. The horse lovers had their pipelines: the telephone and email. The sledders had theirs: the Internet forum and Glenn Daykin's shop. Over coffee, at Spin Drift's long black counter, information (and misinformation) about the lost horses would be shared then spread around McBride and up and down the Robson Valley.

"People think sledders are rednecks," says Barry Walline. "I get it all the time. A lot of people don't like snowmobilers. But the sledding community did step up. What they did made the snowmobile community look good. More respectable than they're commonly perceived. They made McBride look good."

Ray agreed. "This wasn't about the value of horses. You might get $75 for them at the meat plant. The rescue proved to the owner that the horses could be rescued." This was a recurring theme among valley folk. That someone had left the horses on the mountain seemed to imply that getting them off was impossible. For locals, this was a challenge—a gauntlet had been thrown down, and the Robson Valley responded. When it later became clear around McBride that the owner of those horses had expressed doubt that anyone here would help him retrieve his animals, it was viewed as an insult.

Trudy Frisk, the author of an online column on a popular Canadian website called cowboylife.com, wrote eloquently about the rescue in a piece she called "It Takes a Valley." Writing in January of 2009, she remarked on the let's-just-get-it-done attitude that governed what happened on the mountain:

> . . . they hadn't formed a committee, drafted
> a mission statement, applied for a government grant
> and ensured that the shovelling groups were gender
> balanced. They just voluntarily went out in the cold
> and dark, spending time and money to rescue two
> strange horses, horses which didn't belong to them or
> to anybody they knew. Those who couldn't actively dig
> supported the rescue in many other ways; the entire
> valley was involved.

Sundance, July 2010.

Belle, June 2010.

ACKNOWLEDGMENTS

I owe great thanks to my husband and best friend, Marc Lavigne, who was an incredible emotional support to me throughout the entire rescue of Belle and Sundance as well as the writing of this book. Marc read through the various stages of the manuscript and provided important feedback while helping me refresh my memory.

I am much indebted to my co-author, Lawrence Scanlan, who was fascinated by the story of the two rescued horses as soon as he heard it. Larry flew to Dunster to meet with me and many of the volunteers a few months after the rescue; he then worked tirelessly on the manuscript with me for almost two years. I wouldn't have been able to write this book without him.

To my literary agent, Jackie Kaiser of Westwood Creative Artists, thank you for having a vision and believing in this story from day one. You opened up a whole new world to me.

Sincere thanks to everyone at HarperCollins: publisher Iris Tupholme, for her belief in this story; my editor, Kate Cassaday, for setting the bar high; managing editor Noelle Zitzer and production editor Sarah Howden for keeping us all on track; copy editor Cathy Witlox for fine-tuning the manuscript; Lisa Bettencourt for her graphic design talents; and my publicist, Emma Ingram, for her guidance.

Sincere thanks goes out as well to everyone at the Perseus Books Group: my U.S. editor Merloyd Lawrence, senior project editor Annie Lenth, managing editor Fred Francis, publicist Lara Hrabota and art director Jonathan Sainsbury.

I would like to thank Kim Gilbeau, Gordon Jeck, Reg Marek, Frank Peebles, Glen Stanley, Carla Trask and Catie Ward for the use of their photos.

I thank my friend Monika Brown for never giving up on the two horses, even when they were believed to be dead, and for her emotional support throughout the entire rescue.

I would also like to thank Sara Olofsson for answering my desperate plea for help when I first found out about the two starving horses and for being a big supporter of this book from day one.

To my family, thank you for always believing in me and backing me in all my endeavours.

And last but not least, a heartfelt thank-you to everyone who participated in the rescue of Belle and Sundance, whether on the mountain or off it. There were more than fifty people—too many names to mention. Thanks as well to everyone who shared their stories. Without you, this book wouldn't have come to be.

PHOTO CREDITS

PHOTO CREDITS

Page 169: Carla Trask

Page 172: Marc Lavigne

Page 178: Carla Trask

Page 185: Frank Peebles, *Prince George Citizen*

Page 191: Falling Star Ranch*

Page 193: Catie Ward

Page 206: Falling Star Ranch*

Page 209: Falling Star Ranch*

Page 214: Catie Ward

Page 215: Birgit Stutz

Pictures provided by Falling Star Ranch were photographed by various people using Birgit Stutz's camera.

ABOUT THE AUTHORS

BIRGIT STUTZ, journalist, riding instructor and horse trainer, was a key member of the rescue team. She lives on Falling Star Ranch near McBride in northeastern British Columbia together with her husband, 13 horses, six cats and a dog.

LAWRENCE SCANLAN, based in Kingston, Ontario, is the author of several books about horses, including *The Horse God Built: The Untold Story of Secretariat, the World's Greatest Racehorse*. His most recent book is *A Year of Living Generously*.